Churchill's "Iron Curtain" Speech
Fifty Years Later

# Churchill's "Iron Curtain" Speech
# Fifty Years Later

Edited by James W. Muller

*With assistance from the Churchill Center*

University of Missouri Press
Columbia and London

Copyright ©1999 by
The Curators of the University of Missouri
University of Missouri Press, Columbia, Missouri 65201
Printed and bound in the United States of America
All rights reserved
5  4  3  2  1    03  02  01  00  99


**Library of Congress Cataloging–in–Publication Data**

Churchill's Iron Curtain speech fifty years later / edited by James W.
Muller ; with assistance from the Churchill Center.
    p.   cm.
  Includes index.
  ISBN  0-8262-1247-6  (alk.  paper)
  1.  World politics—1945–  2.  Churchill, Winston, Sir,  1874–1965.
Sinews of peace.   I.  Muller, James W., 1953–   . II.  Churchill
Center, Washington, D.C.
D843.C5295   1999
909.82—dc21                                                    99-35267
                                            CIP


∞ ™ This paper meets the requirements of the
American National Standard for Permanence of Paper
for Printed Library Materials, Z39.48, 1984.

Designer: Stephanie Foley
Typesetter: Crane Compositon, Inc.
Printer and Binder: Thomson-Shore, Inc.
Typefaces: Galliard

*To Martin Gilbert*

The Churchill Center
*Washington, D.C.*

The March 1996 colloquium that gave rise to this book was organized in collaboration with the Winston Churchill Memorial and Library at Westminster College in Fulton, Missouri, by the Churchill Center, formally constituted in 1995 under the patronage of the Lady Soames, D.B.E., with more than six hundred founding members. The Churchill Center is an international non-profit organization that encourages the study of Sir Winston Churchill's life and thought; fosters research on his speeches, writings, and deeds; advances knowledge of his example as a statesman; and, by programs of teaching and publishing, imparts that learning to men, women, and young people around the world.

# Contents

꩜ *Preface*

JAMES W. MULLER

From his days as a schoolboy, when he was fasci-
nated by lectures and learned his father's
speeches by heart, Winston Churchill aspired to
oratory. As he tells us in his autobiography, he
delivered his first speech while still a cadet at
Sandhurst, and his first address to an organized
political meeting came soon afterward. During
his years as a soldier in India he explored the
power of public speaking in an unpublished article, "The Scaffolding of Rhetoric," and in his
only novel, *Savrola*. His speeches advanced his
political career as he sought election to the
House of Commons, and after his victory in
1900 a speaking tour made him financially independent for several years. When he took his seat
in Parliament, the young man's speeches gained
the attention of the House and laid the foundations for his career as a minister.

Churchill was quick at repartee and excelled
at impromptu remarks, but success as an orator
did not come without effort. Not only did he
take lessons to overcome his difficulty in pro-
nouncing sibilants, but also, after losing his
thread in an early address to the House of Commons, he settled into the habit of preparing
speeches word for word and learning them by
heart. Memoirs by associates attest to the pains

he took in writing speeches and to the way they commanded his attention, to the exclusion of all else, for days before he spoke.

Decades of public speaking, in Parliament and out-of-doors, prepared Churchill for his lonely warnings against the Nazi menace during the 1930s, culminating in his address after the 1938 Munich Agreement, and for the wartime speeches that roused listeners far and near, who discerned in him the formidable epitome of the British spirit. Churchill's speeches as prime minister from 1940 to 1945 did more than define the Second World War for his audience: they united English-speaking peoples around the world in appreciation of their common heritage of liberty and in a firm resolve to uphold it against tyranny. More than half a century after the end of that war, they remain extraordinarily evocative, even for people too young to have gathered round the wireless to hear them in the 1940s. Churchill's warning that he could offer nothing but "blood, toil, tears and sweat," his exhortation to make the summer of 1940 Britain's "finest hour," and his praise of the airmen in the Battle of Britain—"never in the field of human conflict was so much owed by so many to so few"—earned a lasting place in English rhetoric, and helped win him the Nobel Prize for Literature in 1953.

But Churchill's most famous speech was given after the Second World War, after his party's defeat in 1945, at a small college in the American heartland that became, for one day, the center of the world. Churchill delivered "The Sinews of Peace"—commonly remembered for its description of the "iron curtain" that had descended across Europe—in the presence of President Truman on March 5, 1946, at Westminster College in Fulton, Missouri. Half a century later, the speech is worth rereading for its own sake, but also because it provides a window into Churchill's statesmanship.

To suggest only a glimpse of what one might see through that window, the practical importance of distinguishing friends from enemies in politics was recognized by political philosophers from the beginning: Plato made it a theme of his *Republic*. Democracy depends on statesmen with the prudence to discern, and the rhetorical powers to convey to their fellow citizens, who their friends and enemies are. In his eightieth-birthday speech to Parliament in 1954, Churchill disclaimed responsibility for winning the Second World War: the nation, he said, had the lion's heart, and it fell to him only to provide the roar; but he also hoped he had been able to suggest to the lion the right places to use his claws.

The twentieth century has witnessed in communism and Nazism two of the worst tyrannies ever known to man. But most twentieth-century statesmen, like their fellow citizens susceptible to the specious allure of ideology from the Left or the Right, have been more eager to oppose tyranny on one side than on the other. For too long, their own sympathies made them friendlier to communism or Nazism than they should have been. It is to Churchill's credit that he stood apart from this temptation and steadfastly opposed both kinds of tyranny, well before they were generally abhorred.

In the aftermath of the First World War, Churchill tried to "strangle Bolshevism in its cradle," taking the lead in the postwar Allied effort to topple the new regime during the Russian civil war, so his anticommunist credentials were not in doubt. But he also showed breathtaking flexibility and a clear recognition of the main threat when he made common cause with the Soviets as soon as Hitler attacked Russia. To the charge that he was too friendly to Stalin, Churchill retorted that if Hitler marched into hell, he would at least refer favorably to the devil in the House of Commons. In Britain and America, this wartime propinquity fostered fellow feeling toward their Soviet ally, and by 1946 democratic citizens on both sides of the Atlantic had begun to think of communist Russia as a friend. In his speech at Fulton, Churchill again showed breathtaking flexibility and a clear recognition of the main threat, reminding them that true friendship must be reserved for countries that share a common love of liberty.

Fifty years later, scholars and admirers of Winston Churchill returned to Westminster College to discuss the "Iron Curtain" speech and to hear another former prime minister, Margaret Thatcher, assess the situation of the English-speaking peoples in the era after the cold war. This book is the fruit of that March 1996 gathering at Fulton.

Churchill's "Iron Curtain" speech, reprinted from his book of postwar speeches but corrected according to his exact words at Fulton, is the prologue to the book. Subsequent chapters consider the speech from the viewpoints of history, philosophy, politics, and rhetoric, referring to the speech parenthetically by the prologue's page numbers. In the first chapter, the British historian John Ramsden, drawing on unpublished evidence in the Churchill Papers and elsewhere, investigates Churchill's intention in giving the speech and the extent of cooperation from the British and American governments. Ramsden's claim that Churchill's speech was the leading edge of a concerted change in Anglo-American policy toward Russia finds support in the second chapter, in which the American historian Paul A. Rahe traces the roots of Churchill's message in the Fulton speech to his earlier judgments of the Soviet Union and to Churchill's meeting with Truman the month before. In the third chapter, the American political scientist Daniel J. Mahoney investigates the political philosophy behind the Fulton speech, showing how Churchill's insistence on "Arms and the Covenant" avoids the twin shoals of excessive realism or moralism.

The fourth chapter, by the American author Spencer Warren, accounts for Churchill's approach to the challenge posed by the Soviet Union by describing his philosophy of international politics: a philosophy that recommended clear superiority rather than a precarious balance of power, and a prudent regard for hard facts rather than utopian theories and experiments. In the fifth chapter, the American political scientist Larry P. Arnn explains that Churchill's speech teaches Americans to shoulder the burdens of their defense in the post–cold war world. The sixth chapter, by the American political scientist Patrick J. C. Powers, considers Churchill's speech to explore the possibilities and limits of rhetorical statesmanship in modern democracy. Lady Thatcher's semicentennial speech, which affords a striking practical instance of that statesmanship, serves as epilogue to the book.

The commemoration of "The Sinews of Peace" on its fiftieth anniversary was arranged by the Churchill Center, with help from the Winston S. Churchill Memorial and Library at Westminster College. Participants with me in the semicentennial colloquium on Churchill's "Iron Curtain" speech were Daniel J. Mahoney, Paul A. Rahe, John Ramsden (in residence at Westminster College in 1995-1996 as Robertson Visiting Professor of British History), and Spencer Warren. The liveliness of the discussion at the colloquium suggested the idea for this book. Larry P. Arnn and Patrick J. C. Powers did not attend the colloquium at Fulton but were invited to contribute chapters afterward.

Our hosts at Fulton were James F. Traer, then President of Westminster College, and Judith N. Pugh, then former Director of the Churchill Memorial and Library. To them, and to Parker H. Lee III, former Executive Director of the Churchill Center, we visitors to Westminster College and the other contributing authors owe thanks for arranging the commemoration and colloquium that gave birth to this book. The editor is grateful to Warren M. Hollrah, Curator of Education at the Churchill Memorial and Library, for advice on illustrations; to Scott N. Porter for providing his historic photograph of Churchill and Truman at Fulton; to Gail Greenly of the Churchill Center for secretarial assistance; to fellow Governors of the Churchill Center, and especially to its President, Richard M. Langworth, for steady support; to George D. Mohr for help with proofreading; and to the contributing authors for patience and diligence in preparing this book for publication.

# References to the Official Biography

The official biography is Randolph S. Churchill and Martin Gilbert, *Winston S. Churchill*, eight volumes and sixteen companion volumes to date (London: Heinemann, 1966– ). The first two volumes were penned by Churchill's son and the rest by his successor. In addition to its intrinsic merit as a complete and judicious story of Winston Churchill's life, the official biography has become an indispensable source, along with Churchill's own speeches and writings, for all further research. References to the work have been made by many different methods, often prolix, incomplete, or confusing; in this book we follow a consistent, economical, and reliable method first used in James W. Muller, ed., *Churchill as Peacemaker* (New York: Woodrow Wilson Center Press and Cambridge University Press, 1997), recommending it to others in the hope that it may be generally adopted.

We cite the official biography as *"WSC"* by volume and page number, for example, *WSC* VIII 180–206. The biography is complete in eight main volumes, but each main volume also has a set of two or three companion volumes to attend it. Thus far, the companion volumes have carried the story through the sixth main volume; about seven more such volumes are planned. These volumes are indicated by "C" following the number of the main volume they accompany, for example, *WSC* I C 788–91. Page numbers for the companion volumes run consecutively through each of the first four sets. Beginning with the fifth set, however, each companion volume is paginated separately, so these volumes are distinguished by a parenthetical number preceding the page number, for example, *WSC* VI C (1) 191–95.

References in this book are to the British edition cited above. The official biography has also been published in the United States (Boston: Houghton Mifflin, 1966–1988; New York: Norton, 1993– ); pagination of the American edition is the same as the British edition except in the first two main volumes.

An unofficial appendix to the official biography is Martin Gilbert, *Churchill: A Life* (London: Heinemann, 1991); the American edition (New York: Henry Holt, 1991) has the same pagination.

Churchill's "Iron Curtain" Speech
Fifty Years Later

## The Sinews of Peace

WINSTON S. CHURCHILL

President McCluer, ladies and gentlemen, and last, but certainly not least, President of the United States of America,

I am very glad, indeed, to come to Westminster College this afternoon, and I am complimented that you should give me a degree from an institution whose reputation has been so solidly established. The name "Westminster" somehow or other seems familiar to me. I feel as if I'd heard of it before. Indeed, now that I come to think of it, it was at Westminster that I received a very large part of my education in politics, dialectic, rhetoric, and one or two other things. So in fact we have both been educated at the same, or similar, or, at any rate, kindred establishments.

It is also an honour, ladies and gentlemen, perhaps almost unique, for a private visitor to be introduced to an academic audience by the President of the United States. Amid his heavy burdens, duties, and responsibilities—unsought but not recoiled from—the President has travelled a thousand miles to dignify and magnify our meeting here to-day and to give me an opportunity of addressing this kindred nation, as well as my own countrymen across the ocean, and perhaps some other countries too. The President has told you that it is his wish, as I am sure it is yours,

1

that I should have full liberty to give my true and faithful counsel in these anxious and baffling times. I shall certainly avail myself of this freedom, and feel the more right to do so because any private ambitions I may have cherished in my younger days have been satisfied beyond my wildest dreams. Let me, however, make it clear that I have no official mission or status of any kind. I speak only for myself. There is nothing here but what you see.

I can therefore allow my mind, with the experience of a lifetime, to play over the problems which beset us on the morrow of our absolute victory in arms, and to try to make sure with what strength I have that what has been gained with so much sacrifice and suffering shall be preserved for the future glory and safety of mankind.

Ladies and gentlemen, the United States stands at this time at the pinnacle of world power. It is a solemn moment for the American Democracy. For with primacy in power is also joined an awe-inspiring accountability to the future. If, as you look around you—if you look around you, you must feel not only the sense of duty done but also you must feel anxiety lest you fall below the level of achievement. Opportunity is here now, clear and shining for both our countries. To reject it or ignore it or fritter it away will bring upon us all the long reproaches of the after-time. It is necessary that constancy of mind, persistency of purpose, and the grand simplicity of decision shall rule and guide the conduct of the English-speaking peoples in peace as they did in war. We must, and I believe we shall, prove ourselves equal to this severe requirement.

President McCluer, when American military men approach some serious situation they are wont to write at the head of their directive the words "over-all strategic concept." There is wisdom in this, as it leads to clarity of thought. What then is the over-all strategic concept which we should inscribe to-day? It is nothing less than the safety and welfare, the freedom and progress, of all the homes and families of all the men and women in all the lands. And here I speak particularly of the myriad cottage or apartment homes where the wage-earner strives amid the accidents and difficulties of life to guard his wife and children from privation and bring the family up in the fear of the Lord, or upon ethical conceptions which often play their potent part.

To give security to these countless homes, they must be shielded from the two gaunt marauders, war and tyranny. We all know the frightful disturbance in which the ordinary family is plunged when the curse of war swoops down upon the breadwinner and those for whom he works and contrives. The awful ruin of Europe, with all its vanished glories, and of large parts of Asia glares us in the eyes. When the designs of wicked men or the aggressive urge of mighty States dissolve over large areas the frame of civilized society, humble folk are confronted with difficulties with which they cannot cope. For them all is distorted, all is broken, all is even ground to pulp.

When I stand here this quiet afternoon I shudder to visualize what is actually happening to millions now and what is going to happen in this period when famine stalks the earth. None can compute what has been called "the unestimated sum of human pain." Our supreme task and duty is to guard the homes of the common people from the horrors and miseries of another war. We are all agreed on that.

Our American military colleagues, after having proclaimed their "over-all strategic concept" and computed available resources, always proceed to the next step—namely, the method. Here again there is widespread agreement. A world organization has already been erected for the prime purpose of preventing war. UNO, the successor of the League of Nations, with the decisive addition of the United States and all that that means, is already at work. We must make sure that its work is fruitful, that it is a reality and not a sham, that it is a force for action and not merely a frothing of words, that it is a true temple of peace in which the shields of many nations can some day be hung up, and not merely a cockpit in a Tower of Babel. Before we cast away the solid assurances of national armaments for self-preservation we must be certain that our temple is built, not upon shifting sands or quagmires, but upon the rock. Anyone can see with his eyes open that our path will be difficult and also long, but if we persevere together as we did in the two World Wars— though not, alas, in the interval between them—I cannot doubt that we shall achieve our common purpose in the end.

I have, however, a definite and practical proposal to make for action. Courts and magistrates may be set up but they cannot function without sheriffs and constables. The United Nations Organization must immediately begin to be equipped with an international armed force. In such a matter we can only go step by step, but we must begin now. I propose that each of the Powers and States should be invited to dedicate a certain number of air squadrons to the service of the world organization. These squadrons would be trained and prepared in their own countries, but would move around in rotation from one country to another. They would wear the uniforms of their own countries but with different badges. They would not be required to act against their own nation, but in other respects they would be directed by the world organization. This might be started on a modest scale and it would grow as confidence grew. I wished to see this done after the First World War, and I devoutly trust that it may be done forthwith.

It would nevertheless, ladies and gentlemen, be wrong and imprudent to entrust the secret knowledge or experience of the atomic bomb, which the United States, Great Britain, and Canada now share, to the world organization, while it is still in its infancy. It would be criminal madness to cast it adrift in this still agitated and un-united world. No one in any country has slept less well in their beds because this knowledge, and the method and the raw materials to apply it, are at present largely retained in American hands. I do not believe we should all have slept so soundly had the positions been reversed and some Communist or neo-Fascist State monopolized for the time being these dread agencies. The fear of them alone might easily have been used to enforce totalitarian systems upon the free democratic world, with consequences appalling to human imagination. God has willed that this shall not be and we have at least a breathing space to set our house in order before this peril has to be encountered: and even then, if no effort is spared, we should still possess so formidable a superiority as to impose effective deterrents upon its employment, or threat of employment, by others. Ultimately, when the essential brotherhood of man is truly embodied and expressed in a world organization with all the necessary practical safeguards to make it effective, these powers would naturally be confided to that world organization.

Now I come to the second of the two marauders—to the second danger which threatens the cottage home and ordinary people—

namely, tyranny. We cannot be blind to the fact that the liberties enjoyed by individual citizens throughout the United States and throughout the British Empire are not valid in a considerable number of countries, some of which are very powerful. In these States control is enforced upon the common people by various kinds of all-embracing police governments, to a degree which is overwhelming, and contrary to every principle of democracy. The power of the State is exercised without restraint, either by dictators or by compact oligarchies operating through a privileged party and a political police. It is not our duty at this time when difficulties are so numerous to interfere forcibly in the internal affairs of countries which we have not conquered in war. But we must never cease to proclaim in fearless tones the great principles of freedom and the rights of man which are the joint inheritance of the English-speaking world and which through Magna Carta, the Bill of Rights, the Habeas Corpus, trial by jury, the English common law find their most famous expression in the American Declaration of Independence.

All this means that the people of any country have the right, and should have the power by constitutional action, by free unfettered elections, with secret ballot, to choose or change the character or form of government under which they dwell; that freedom of speech and thought should reign; that courts of justice, independent of the executive, unbiased by any party, should administer laws which have received the broad assent of large majorities or are consecrated by time and custom. Here are the title deeds of freedom which should lie in every cottage home. Here is the message of the British and American peoples to mankind. Let us preach what we practise—let us practise what we preach.

Sir, I have now stated the two great dangers which menace the homes of the people: War and Tyranny. I have not yet spoken of poverty and privation which are in many cases the prevailing anxiety. But if the dangers of war and tyranny are removed, there is no doubt that science and co-operation can bring in the next few years, certainly in the next few decades, to the world, newly taught in the sharpening school of war, an expansion of material well-being beyond anything that has yet occurred in human experience. Now, at this sad and breathless moment, we are plunged in the hunger and distress which are the aftermath of our stupendous struggle; but this will pass and may pass quickly, and there is no reason except human folly or sub-human crime which should deny to all the nations the inauguration and enjoyment of an age of plenty. I have often used words which I learned fifty years ago from a great Irish-American orator, a friend of mine, Mr. Bourke Cockran, "There is enough for all. The earth is a generous mother; she will provide in plentiful abundance food for all her children if they will but cultivate her soil in justice and in peace." So far I feel that we are in full agreement.

Now, while still pursuing the method of realizing our over-all strategic concept, I come to the crux of what I have travelled here to say. Neither the sure prevention of war, nor the continuous rise of world organization will be gained without what I have called the fraternal association of the English-speaking peoples. This means a special relationship between the British Commonwealth and Empire and the United States of America. Ladies and gentlemen, this is no time for generalities, and I will venture to be precise. Fraternal association requires not only the growing friendship and mutual understanding between our two vast but kindred systems of society, but the continuance of the intimate relation between our military advisers, leading to common study of potential dangers, the similarity of weapons and manuals of instruction, and to the interchange of officers and cadets at technical colleges. It should carry with it the continuance of the present facilities for mutual security by the joint use of all Naval and Air Force bases in the possession of either country all over the world. This would perhaps double the mobility of the American Navy and Air Force. It would greatly expand that of the British Empire Forces and it might well lead, if and as the world calms down, to important financial savings. Already we use together a large number of islands; more may well be entrusted to our joint care in the near future.

The United States has already a Permanent Defence Agreement with the Dominion of Canada, which is so devotedly attached to the British Commonwealth and Empire. This Agreement is more effective than many of those which have often been made under formal alliances. This principle should be extended to all the British Commonwealths with full reciprocity. Thus, whatever happens, and thus only, shall we be secure ourselves and able to work together for the high and simple causes that are dear to us and bode no ill to any. Eventually there may come—I feel eventually there will come—the principle of common citizenship, but that we may be content to leave to destiny, whose outstretched arm many of us can already clearly see.

There is, however, an important question we must ask ourselves. Would a special relationship between the United States and the British Commonwealth be inconsistent with our over-riding loyalties to the World Organization? I reply that, on the contrary, it is probably the only means by which that organization will achieve its full stature and strength. There are already the special United States relations with Canada which I have just mentioned, and there are the relations between the United States and the South American Republics. We have also—we British have also our twenty years' Treaty of Collaboration and Mutual Assistance with Soviet Russia. I agree with Mr. Bevin, the Foreign Secretary of Great Britain, that it might well be a fifty years' Treaty so far as we are concerned. We aim at nothing but mutual assistance and collaboration with Russia. We have an alliance—the British have an alliance with Portugal unbroken since the year 1384, and which produced fruitful results at a critical moment in the recent war. None of these clash with the general interest of a world agreement, or a world organization; on the contrary they help it. "In my father's house are many mansions." Special associations between members of the United Nations which have no aggressive point against any other country, which harbour no design incompatible with the Charter of the United Nations, far from being harmful, are beneficial and, as I believe, indispensable.

I spoke earlier, ladies and gentlemen, of the Temple of Peace. Workmen from all countries must build that temple. If two of the workmen know each other particularly well and are old friends, if their families are intermingled, if they have "faith in each other's purpose, hope in each other's future and charity towards each other's shortcomings"—to quote some good words I read here the other day—why cannot they work together at the common task as friends and partners? Why can they not share their tools and thus increase each other's working powers? Indeed they must do so or else the temple may not be built, or, being built, it may collapse, and we shall all be proved again unteachable and have to go and try to learn again for a third time in a school of war, incomparably more rigorous than that from which we have just been released. The dark ages may return, the Stone Age may return on the gleaming wings of science, and what might now shower immeasurable material blessings upon mankind may even bring about its total destruction. Beware, I say; time may be short. Do not let us take the course of allowing events to drift along until it is too late. If there is to be a fraternal association of the kind I have described, with all the extra strength and security which both our countries can derive from it, let us make sure that that great fact is known to the world, and that it plays its part in steadying and stabilizing the foundations of peace. There is the path of wisdom. Prevention is better than cure.

A shadow has fallen upon the scenes so lately lighted by the Allied victory. Nobody knows what Soviet Russia and its Communist international organization intends to do in the immediate future, or what are the limits, if any, to their expansive and proselytizing tendencies. I have a strong admiration and regard for the valiant Russian people and for my wartime comrade, Marshal Stalin. There is deep sympathy and goodwill in Britain—and I doubt not here also—towards the peoples of all the Russias and a resolve to persevere through many differences and rebuffs in establishing lasting friendships. We understand the Russian need to be secure on her western frontiers by the removal of all possibility of German aggression. We welcome Russia to her rightful place among the leading nations of the world. We welcome her flag upon the seas. Above all, we welcome, or should welcome, constant, frequent and growing contacts between the Russian people and our own peoples on both sides of the Atlantic. It is my duty, however, for I am sure you would not wish me to—not to state the facts as I see them to you, it is my duty to place before you certain facts about the present position in Europe.

From Stettin in the Baltic to Trieste in the Adriatic, an iron curtain has descended across the Continent. Behind that line lie all the capitals of the ancient states of Central and Eastern Europe. Warsaw, Berlin, Prague, Vienna, Budapest, Belgrade, Bucharest and Sofia, all these famous cities and the populations around them lie in what I must call the Soviet sphere, and all are subject in one form or another, not only to Soviet influence but to a very high and, in some cases, increasing measure of control from Moscow. Athens alone — Greece with its immortal glories — is free to decide its future at an election under British, American and French observation. The Russian-dominated Polish Government has been encouraged to make enormous and wrongful inroads upon Germany, and mass expulsions of millions of Germans on a scale grievous and undreamed-of are now taking place. The Communist parties, which were very small in all these Eastern States of Europe, have been raised to pre-eminence and power far beyond their numbers and are seeking everywhere to obtain totalitarian control. Police governments are prevailing in nearly every case, and so far, except in Czechoslovakia, there is no true democracy.

Turkey and Persia are both profoundly alarmed and disturbed at the claims which are being made upon them and at the pressure being exerted by the Moscow Government. An attempt is being made by the Russians in Berlin to build up a quasi-Communist party in their zone of Occupied Germany by showing special favours to groups of left-wing German leaders. At the end of the fighting last June, the American and British Armies withdrew westwards, in accordance with an earlier agreement, to a depth at some points of 150 miles upon a front of nearly four hundred miles, in order to allow our Russian allies to occupy this vast expanse of territory which the Western Democracies had conquered.

If now the Soviet Government tries, by separate action, to build up a pro-Communist Germany in their areas, this will cause new serious difficulties in the American and British zones, and will give the defeated Germans the power of putting themselves up to auction between the Soviets and the Western Democracies. Whatever conclusions may be drawn from these facts — and facts they are — this is certainly not the Liberated Europe we fought to build up. Nor is it one which contains the essentials of permanent peace.

The safety of the world, ladies and gentlemen, requires a new unity in Europe, from which no nation should be permanently outcast. It is from the quarrels of the strong parent races in Europe that the world wars we have witnessed, or which occurred in former

times, have sprung. Twice in our own lifetime we have seen the
United States, against their wishes and their traditions, against arguments, the force of which it is impossible—the force of which it is
impossible not to comprehend, twice we have seen them drawn by
irresistible forces into these wars in time to secure the victory of the
good cause, but only after frightful slaughter and devastation have
occurred. Twice the United States has had to send several millions of
its young men across the Atlantic to find the war; but now war can
find any nation, wherever it may dwell, between dusk and dawn.
Surely we should work with conscious purpose for a grand pacifica-
tion of Europe, within the structure of the United Nations and in accordance with our Charter. That I feel is a—opens a course of policy
of very great importance.

In front of the iron curtain which lies across Europe are other
causes for anxiety. In Italy the Communist Party is seriously ham-
pered by having to support the Communist-trained Marshal Tito's
claims to former Italian territory at the head of the Adriatic. Nevertheless the future of Italy hangs in the balance. Again one cannot
imagine a regenerated Europe without a strong France. All my public life I have worked for a strong France and I never lost faith in her
destiny, even in the darkest hours. I will not lose faith now. However,
in a great number of countries, far from the Russian frontiers and
throughout the world, Communist fifth columns are established and
work in complete unity and absolute obedience to the directions
they receive from the Communist centre. Except in the British Commonwealth and in the United States where Communism is in its infancy, the Communist parties or fifth columns constitute a growing
challenge and peril to Christian civilization. These are sombre facts
for anyone to have to recite on the morrow of a victory gained by so
much splendid comradeship in arms and in the cause of freedom and
democracy; but we should be most unwise not to face them squarely
while time remains.

The outlook is also anxious in the Far East and especially in
Manchuria. The Agreement which was made at Yalta, to which I was
a party, was extremely favourable to Soviet Russia, but it was made at
a time when no one could say that the German war might not extend
all through the summer and autumn of 1945 and when the Japanese

war was expected by the best judges to last for a further 18 months from the end of the German war. In this country you are all so well-informed about the Far East, and such devoted friends of China, that I do not need to expatiate on the situation there.

I have, however, felt bound to portray the shadow which, alike in the west and in the east, falls upon the world. I was a minister at the time of the Versailles Treaty and a close friend of Mr. Lloyd George, who was the head of the British delegation at that time. I did not myself agree with many things that were done, but I have a very strong impression in my mind of that situation, and I find it painful to contrast it with that which prevails now. In those days there were high hopes and unbounded confidence that the wars were over and that the League of Nations would become all-powerful. I do not see or feel that same confidence or even the same hopes in the haggard world at the present time.

On the other hand, ladies and gentlemen, I repulse the idea that a new war is inevitable; still more that it is imminent. It is because I am sure that our fortunes are still in our own hands and that we hold the power to save the future, that I feel the duty to speak out now that I have the occasion and the opportunity to do so. I do not believe that Soviet Russia desires war. What they desire is the fruits of war and the indefinite expansion of their power and doctrines. But what we have to consider here to-day, while time remains, is the permanent prevention of war and the establishment of conditions of freedom and democracy as rapidly as possible in all countries. Our difficulties and dangers will not be removed by closing our eyes to them. They will not be removed by mere waiting to see what happens; nor will they be removed by a policy of appeasement. What is needed is a settlement, and the longer this is delayed, the more difficult it will be and the greater our dangers will become.

From what I have seen of our Russian friends and Allies during the war, I am convinced that there is nothing they admire so much as strength, and there is nothing for which they have less respect than for weakness, especially military weakness. For that—for that reason the old doctrine of a balance of power is unsound. We cannot afford, if we can help it, to work on narrow margins, offering temptations to a trial of strength. If the Western Democracies stand together in strict adherence to the principles of the United Nations Charter, their influence for furthering those principles will be immense and no one is likely to molest them. If, however, they become divided or falter in their duty and if these all-important years are allowed to slip away, then indeed catastrophe may overwhelm us all.

Last time I saw it all coming and I cried aloud to my own fellow-countrymen and to the world, but no one paid any attention. Up till the year 1933, or even 1935, Germany might have been saved from the awful fate which has overtaken her and we might all have been spared the miseries Hitler let loose upon mankind. There never was a war in history easier to prevent by timely action than the one which has just desolated such great areas of the globe. It could have been prevented in my belief without the firing of a single shot, and Germany might be powerful, prosperous and honoured to-day; but no one would listen and one by one we were all sucked into the awful whirlpool. We surely, ladies and gentlemen: I put it to you, surely, we must not let that happen again. This can only be achieved by reaching now, in 1946—this year, 1946—by reaching a good understanding on all points with Russia under the general authority of the United Nations Organization, and by the maintenance of that good understanding through many peaceful years, by the world instrument, supported by the whole strength of the English-speaking world and all its connections. There is the solution which I respectfully offer to you in this Address to which I have given the title "The Sinews of Peace."

Let no man underrate the abiding power of the British Empire and Commonwealth. Because you see the 46 millions in our island harassed about their food supply, of which they only grow one half, even in wartime, or because we have difficulty in restarting our industries and export trade after six years of passionate war effort, do not suppose we shall not come through these dark years of privation as we have come through the glorious years of agony; do not suppose that half a century from now, you will not see 70 or 80 millions of Britons spread about the world, united in defence of our traditions and our way of life, and of the world causes which you and we espouse. If the population of the English-speaking Commonwealths be added to that of the United States, with all that such co-operation implies in the air, on the sea, all over the globe, and in science and in industry, and in moral force, there will be no quivering, precarious balance of power to offer its temptation to ambition or adventure. On the contrary, there will be an overwhelming assurance of security. If we adhere faithfully to the Charter of the United Nations and walk forward in sedate and sober strength, seeking no one's land or treasure, seeking to lay no arbitrary control upon the thoughts of men; if all British moral and material forces and convictions are joined with your own in fraternal association, the highroads of the future will be clear, not only for us but for all, not only for our time, but for a century to come.

*One* ~

## Mr. Churchill Goes to Fulton

JOHN RAMSDEN

Winston Churchill's journey to the campus of a small college in a remote town in the heart of the United States, Westminster College in Fulton, Missouri, in March 1946, to deliver what is variously known as the "Iron Curtain" speech,[1] the "Sinews of Peace" speech, or just the Fulton speech, has acquired a mythic significance both in evaluations of the great man's postwar career and in investigations of the point at which the cold war went into superfreeze.

For Churchill, the speech at Fulton was the

1. In view of recent comments on the paradox that Churchill should in March 1946 have become more famous for using the phrase "iron curtain," which had allegedly originated from Joseph Goebbels or the Nazi minister of finance, it may be a good idea to give the real background. "Iron curtain" was first used by the queen of Belgium to describe the division of her country by the German invasion of 1914, and first applied to Russia by the British socialist Ethel Snowden. Churchill borrowed it to describe Russia after the 1917 revolution in *The World Crisis*, and thus used it long before the Nazis. In 1944–1945 it was fairly widely applied to Eastern Europe after the advance of the Red Army, by the *Times* (London) in an editorial as well as by Germans. At that time Churchill also used it in a telegram to Truman, and (in this version "an iron fence") he had even used it to Stalin face-to-face (and received the reply, "All fairy stories!"). There is nothing surprising in Churchill in the 1940s giving new fame to a well-worn phrase, for the same can be said of "blood, toil, tears, and sweat" (originating with John Donne and used by Byron, among others) and of "Never ... has much been owed ... to so many" (which Churchill himself had been using pretty continuously ever since the Edwardian period). The

first of a series of major orations, almost all on international affairs, that kept his name and his reputation alive during his six years out of office after his defeat in 1945. It would be followed by similar international triumphs at Zurich, Strasbourg, Boston, and The Hague so that journalists who followed him on the international circuit found that he remained better known across Europe and in the United States than were either the British prime minister or the foreign secretary.[2] These successes, beginning with the extraordinary attention paid by the international community to the purely personal opinions he expressed at Fulton, helped both to persuade Churchill against retirement and to provide the platform on which his comeback could be staged.[3]

The speech has a quite different significance in the historiography of international relations, where it tends to be interpreted as a milestone along the way to growing antagonism between the Soviet Union and the West. Whereas it was once generally argued that Churchill alone saw the need for a strong Western response to Russian expansionism, and that his courageous call for such measures at Fulton had itself awakened the sleeping giant of American arms in defense of freedom, more recently historians have rightly pointed to the extent to which American elite opinion was already tending in that direction before Churchill went to Fulton.[4] In support of this

---

editorial introduction to the first edition of the *Oxford Dictionary of Quotations* cited Churchill's wartime radio broadcasts as showing the value of a well-known phrase in improving his rapport with his audience, the impact relying less on novelty than on customer recognition, and commented on the extent to which this all showed Churchill to be soaked in the literary and conversational vernacular of the English-speaking world. For the origins of the other phrases referred to above, see recent editions of *Bartlett's Familiar Quotations*.

2. Arthur Booth, *The True Story of Winston Churchill* (Chicago: Children's Press, 1958), 128. Booth was assigned to follow Churchill on his overseas travels by the Press Association.

3. John Ramsden, inaugural lecture, "'That Will Depend on Who Writes the History': Winston Churchill as His Own Historian" (London: Queen Mary and Westfield College, 1997); for a shortened version, see W. Roger Louis, *Further Adventures with Britannia* (Austin: University of Texas Press, 1998), 241–55.

4. See, for example, Melvyn P. Leffler, *The Specter of Communism: The United States and the Origins of the Cold War, 1917–1953* (New York: Hill and Wang, 1994), 52–53; Martin Walker, *The Cold War* (London: Vintage, 1994), 37–39; Fraser J. Harbutt, *The Iron Curtain: Churchill, America, and the Origins of the Cold War* (New York: Oxford University Press, 1986); Martin McCauley, *The Origins of the Cold War*, 2d ed. (London: Longman, 1995), 73.

view, they cite the gradual shift in the views of President Harry
Truman toward a tougher response to Stalin over the winter of
1945–1946, the insistent reports of Averell Harriman from Europe arguing that action would be all that Stalin would understand, and especially the "long telegram" that George Kennan
was encouraged to send from Moscow in late February 1946, setting out the case for a strong response to Stalin at its most cogent
—and in the words of a man recognized as the State Department's most informed Russianist. Secretary of State Byrnes was
still more reluctant over the impending tilt of policy, and Truman
seemed unwilling to overrule him, but the assumption remains
that, with or without Churchill, the United States would have
shifted its international policy in a tougher direction, and sooner
rather than later.

These two viewpoints do not exactly coincide, though even
without knowledge of the details it is not hard to surmise that
Churchill's personal views and those of Washington's experts on
Soviet affairs may simply have converged, reaching similar conclusions from much the same experience of Russian policy. But all
analyses to date suffer from the same problems. First, Churchill's
visit to Fulton was claimed to be (and was reported as) a purely
personal one, and his speech was prefaced with a clear statement
that he did not speak on behalf of anyone but himself. When the
speech produced a hail of criticism both in Britain and in the
United States, the British and American governments reiterated
that view and officially detached themselves from what Churchill
had said. As a result of these insistent denials, neither Truman nor
Prime Minister Clement Attlee and Foreign Secretary Ernest
Bevin could plausibly claim a share of the credit when after an interval—largely as a result of Russian reactions to the speech, or at
least of Russian actions soon after the speech—Churchill's speech
came to be seen as uniquely prophetic. (By comparison with the
instantaneous debate on Churchill's words, Harriman's opinions
on Russia, Kennan's telegrams, and the other policy influences in
the same direction as the "Iron Curtain" speech did not surface
until memoirs were written and historians added the documents
to the debate years after the event.) Churchill's solo warning

about the threat to freedom posed by Stalin fitted neatly with the reputation that he already had of being uniquely right about Hitler before 1939. And so it passed into the mythology.

But was it true that the Churchill speech was a solo effort, or was it carefully contrived by (or at least with) the British and American governments to achieve a precalculated effect?[5] Was it, in other words, simply convenient for Attlee and Truman to have Churchill go out on a limb at Fulton, given that their complicity could easily be denied if the need arose (as indeed it did)? And how far was Churchill himself aware of his own convenience to others in this process? Only with the recent opening of the Churchill Papers can we even begin to answer that central question.[6]

Second, reactions to the speech have often tended to miss the extent to which his later speech in New York, just ten days after he had spoken at Fulton, readjusted the balance of the policy that he recommended, corrected misunderstandings, and allayed some fears. Even in the short period between those two speeches, between March 5 and 15, 1946, Stalin's violent speech in reaction to what Churchill had said and the actuality of Russian policy in Iran had changed the balance of the argument anyway. We need to establish not only just what Churchill meant to say, but also how he adjusted it quickly in response to a rapidly changing international crisis.

I therefore begin by looking briefly at what the two speeches actually said, and seek to establish whence in Churchill's thinking and previous experience the key concepts came. I then discuss how far the British government was involved in the speech and may be presumed to have shown either foreknowledge or post-facto approval of Churchill's views. Third, I attempt the same exercise with respect to the American government. Finally, I look briefly at the speeches' actual impact on the United States.

5. As argued by Harbutt, *Iron Curtain*, 152 and passim.

6. Churchill's visit to the United States in January–March 1946 produced a dozen specific correspondence and speech files that have survived, as well as documents in many other areas of the collection, and even all this seems not to include most of the three thousand or so letters to him from American citizens. I am grateful to the Master and Fellows of Churchill College for permission to quote from the Churchill Papers.

## Preparing "A Real Message"

It is quite clear that Churchill had seen from the start that the invitation to go to Fulton had given him a wonderful opportunity to bring off something big. He told Truman, "I have a message to deliver to your country and the world," and Truman's reply picked up and repeated the phrase: "I know you have a real message to deliver at Fulton." The speech eventually given was longer than any that Churchill produced over the two years after the war, except the Party Conference oration in October 1946 to reestablish his party leadership, and the preparations for Fulton were on a suitably elaborate scale. He had decided that the original request to give a series of four lectures was too much for him in his exhausted postwar condition, but he grasped that Truman's involvement in the invitation produced an opportunity for a major media event. In advance, Churchill told the president of Westminster College that "in the circumstances, it will be a political pronouncement of considerable importance," and as they left the college gymnasium in which the speech was delivered, he told President McCluer that he hoped he had "started some thinking that will make history."[7] On the train back to Washington, Churchill proclaimed that it had been "the most important speech of my career."[8]

What were the special circumstances, though, that enabled history to be made? In accepting Truman's fairly casual invitation, he committed the president to rather more than had perhaps been intended: "if you...would like me to visit you in your home State and would introduce me, I should feel it my duty—and it would also be a great pleasure—to deliver an address...on the world situation under your aegis." When beginning the speech at Fulton, Churchill not only drew attention to the fact that the president had invited him personally but pointed out that Truman too had traveled more than a thousand miles "to dignify and magnify our meeting." Elaborate plans

7. Churchill to Truman, Jan. 29, 1946, and Truman to Churchill, Feb. 2, 1946, Churchill Papers, at Churchill College, Cambridge [hereafter CP] 2/158; Churchill to Franc McCluer, Jan. 30, 1946, CP 2/230; analysis of speeches, January 1945 to June 1947, June 27, 1947, CP 5/1. William E. Parrish, *Westminster College: An Informal History* (Fulton, Mo.: Westminster College, 1971), 211.
8. Charles Ross diary, Mar. 7, 1946, Harry S. Truman Presidential Library.

had been made for press coverage, the speech was published almost in full by all three of the major press services in the United States, newsreels filmed the speech, and the entire speech was broadcast live, coast-to-coast (and in Canada), on CBS Radio. Because of the importance of the event, however, Churchill did veto television coverage, since he "deprecate[d] complicating the occasion with technical experiments."[9]

In preparation for the big event, Churchill took his personal secretary with him to America, at considerable additional expense both to himself and to his American host Colonel Frank Clarke, for Jo Sturdee alone would be able to give him the experienced support of someone who knew his working habits. This proved important when, as usual, the final version of the speech was produced only at the last moment, for (as Sturdee explained) "on such occasions Mr. Churchill makes alterations and additions on the spur of the moment." Nothing was done to dampen rising interest in the coming speech, but equally Churchill refused all interviews so as not to give away any hint of what he intended to say in Fulton. When asked by reporters in Miami on February 12 whether he had discussed relations with Russia on his recent visit to Truman, Churchill replied, "No comment," and then added with a grin, "I think 'No Comment' is a splendid expression. I am using it again and again." Meanwhile, Truman somewhat disingenuously reassured the more pro-Russian members of the administration by telling them that Churchill's speech would just be "the usual 'hands across the sea' stuff." No other speeches of any importance were arranged for the period between Churchill's arrival in America and the Fulton meeting, though he did agree to several engagements over the following fortnight, in particular to speak in Richmond, Virginia, and in New York, so that his favors would be spread equally across the South, the Midwest, and the Northeast, only the Far West being entirely deprived of his attention. When Westminster College announced early in January that only ticket holders would be allowed to attend, it received within a fortnight fifteen thousand requests for the three

---

9. Speech notes, Fulton speech, Mar. 5, 1946, CP 5/3; Churchill to Truman, Nov. 8, 1945, and Churchill to Franc McCluer, Feb. 5, 1946, CP 2/230.

thousand or so available places, and demand continued to rise over the next six weeks.[10]

Expectations were therefore high when Churchill, following a triumphant motorcade through the city, rose to speak at Fulton on March 5, 1946, and he did not disappoint. In brief, the speech outlined the threat that communism posed to the free world, with pointed descriptions of "police government" under a "privileged party," and he juxtaposed this with the common-law background that had made the Magna Carta, the Bill of Rights, and the United States Declaration of Independence the joint inheritance of the British Commonwealth and the United States. Churchill then explained that "the crux of what I have travelled here to say" was that the prevention of another war at an early date depended entirely on "the fraternal association of the English-speaking peoples. This means a special relationship between the British Commonwealth and Empire and the United States." He argued that the United Nations might develop into a peacemaking court of world opinion, but emphasized that peacemaking requires sheriffs as well as judges, with the English-speaking peoples cast in the role of the law enforcers of the world; he envisaged that as a first step, the joint American-Canadian defense agreement could be extended to the rest of the Commonwealth, but he did not rule out future cooperation, reaching even to common citizenship. Ten days later in New York, by which time he had received heavy attacks both from Stalin and from the British and American Left, Churchill proclaimed that "when I spoke at Fulton...I felt it was necessary for someone in an unofficial position to speak in arresting terms about the present plight of the world." Here came a long pause to increase audience tension as to what he was going to say; then, slowly and with great force, he added, "I do not wish to withdraw or modify a single word." "The only question," he insisted, was whether the United Kingdom and the United States united to prevent a world war "or in the course of that struggle" as

10. Churchill to Col. Clarke, Jan. 1, 1946, CP 2/225; Miss Sturdee to Charles Campbell, Feb. 2, 1946, CP 2/224; Miss Sturdee to Philip Clarke, Feb. 4, 1946, CP 2/224; Halifax to Churchill, Feb. 3, 1946, Hickleton Papers, 4/11 (microfilm at Churchill College); R. H. Pilpel, *Churchill in America* (New York: Harcourt Brace, 1976), 216; Harbutt, *Iron Curtain*, 168; Parrish, *Westminster College*, 201.

in 1941. Nevertheless, at New York, Churchill did tone down some parts of his message and amplify others; he was careful to accept that Russia did not want war, at least "at the present time," and to pay a warm tribute to all that Russians had done in the war against the Nazis, pointing out that if the Russian government managed to forfeit the world's admiration for the Russian people, then the fault would be entirely its own; and he was even more careful than at Fulton to emphasize that he wanted a friendship with the United States that extended to practical cooperation, and not a military alliance. But America's great economic and military power, he insisted, imposed duties and responsibilities that must not be shirked.[11]

## The Origins and Impact of the Speech

Where, then, had these thoughts come from? On the extent of the threat to peace, Churchill's views had certainly shifted over the winter of 1945–1946. In a Commons debate on demobilization in October 1945, he had accepted the government's plans to reduce the armed forces on the basis that "it is common ground that this possibility of a major war may rightly be excluded, at any rate that we have an interlude of peace." Three weeks later he deleted, presumably as too scaremongering, a paragraph from his Commons speech on foreign policy that described the horrors of the recent war and forecast "a period of still more hideous conflict.... One cannot but feel a sense of danger, the menace of vast, descending tribulations." By the time he spoke at Fulton, the equivalent passages remained in the speech, and he took a much darker view of the potential risk of war than he had done in public before. In much the same way, his view of Soviet Russia—or at least what he said about it—darkened over the same period. He had also deleted from his November 7 Commons speech a claim that Truman "would not tolerate wrongly-headed, unfair, tyrannical governments," while adding at the last

11. Speech notes, Fulton, Mar. 5, 1946, and City Banquet in New York, Mar. 15, 1946, CP 5/4.

stage of drafting a reassuring sentence arguing that closer Anglo-American relations did not exclude Russia from friendship with both of them, though in private conversation with Mackenzie King he took a much harder line. Although he again upped the rhetorical level of his anticommunism at Fulton in his references to the "iron curtain" and to "barbarism," he was also ready to retreat somewhat when he spoke again in New York.[12]

On one theme, though, Churchill's argument never wavered, and that was on the necessity for closer working relations between Britain and America, which he invariably saw as both natural and beneficial to world peace; it was perhaps more than coincidental that it was while sailing to America that Churchill resumed work on his *History of the English-Speaking Peoples,* abandoned in 1939. In the Commons on November 7, he had argued that Britain and America "come together naturally" as a result of their linguistic, legal, and literary background, and that on all important issues "the English-speaking peoples of the world are in general agreement." He concluded, "We should fortify in every way our special and friendly connections with the United States, aiming always at a fraternal association for the purposes of common protection and world peace." The Fulton speech did not materially advance that argument, and though it contained the first formal usage of the phrase "special relationship," in November 1945 Churchill had already spoken of "special and friendly connections," and he even used the phrase "special relationship" in that speech, but in the context of Anglo-American-Canadian nuclear cooperation. When at Fulton he applied it to Anglo-American relations in general, the phrase added a subtle appeal to a common kinship to the usual claim of joint self-interest.[13]

And so the theme continued through the winter. Even when addressing the Belgian Senate and Chamber in Brussels on November 16, Churchill felt he had to explain that "it is evident of course that the affairs of Great Britain and the British Commonwealth and Empire are becoming ever more closely interwoven with those of the United States, and that an underlying unity of thought and

12. Speech notes, House of Commons, Oct. 22, 1945, CP 5/1; Speech notes, House of Commons, Nov. 7, 1945, CP 5/2; *WSC* VIII 161.
13. *WSC* VIII 180; Speech notes, House of Commons, Nov. 7, 1945, CP 5/2.

conviction increasingly pervades the English-speaking world." Quite what moral the Belgians were supposed to draw from this was not clear, but some Europeans certainly thought it an alarming sign of Britain turning away from Europe. After he had spoken at Fulton, Churchill received a report from Duff Cooper, the British ambassador in Paris, saying that many Frenchmen were worried that Churchill "had given up France as a lost country which could no longer be of assistance to anyone," and that his hopes "were centred solely on the United States." Frenchmen who entertained such worries would not have been reassured by his reply, which regretted that France had "fallen again into political fatuity" and hoped that the Communists would not win the impending election (in which case Churchill would consider them "ruined for ever," though he trusted "that even a Communist France will not debar me from Monte Carlo"). He concluded with the patronizing hope "that France will shape her destiny in harmony with the two great Western democracies."[14]

In the Commons in December, Churchill was on an even stickier wicket, for the bulk of his own party thought that the Americans had extracted unduly vindictive terms from Britain in negotiations for a postwar loan, and he struggled to prevent Conservatives as a whole from voting against the proposal. Even under these trying circumstances, he made a plea for closer relations, for "united, these two countries can, without the slightest injury to other nations or to themselves, almost double each other's prosperity, and united they can surely double each other's power and safety." Once in America in January 1946, inhibitions disappeared and Churchill's language became more extravagant. In an impromptu address at the University of Miami, he quoted Bismarck as saying that "the most important fact in the world was that the British and American people spoke the same language," and rhapsodized about the "noble inheritance of literature" that "unites us as no such great communities have ever been united before." He was therefore well prepared for the appeal that he made at Fulton, and on this issue there was no modification over the following weeks. At Richmond he said, "In these last years

14. Speech notes, Brussels, Nov. 16, 1945, CP 5/2; Duff Cooper to Churchill, Apr. 2, 1946, and Churchill to Cooper, Apr. 7, 1946, CP 2/5.

of my life there is a message of which I conceive myself to be a bearer. It is a very simple message which can be well understood by the people of both countries. It is that we should stand together.... among the English-speaking peoples of the world there must be the union of hearts based upon conviction and common ideals."[15] And remarkably, for such a quintessential Englishman as Churchill liked to think himself, he made an admission during the train journey to Missouri that would not have gone down at all well if quoted in London; he suddenly said to his fellow card players that there was only one country into which he would now wish to be born, one country that had an unbounded future, and when asked to say which country that was, he exclaimed, "The United States of America."[16]

There was, though, a price for this celebration of everything American, for Churchill called at Fulton and again in New York for America to take up the main burden in the new relationship, a point that he had also made explicitly to Truman in the previous November. "The United States," he wrote, "has reached a pinnacle of glory and power not exceeded by any nation in the history of the world, and with that come not only opportunities literally for saving misguided humanity but also terrible responsibilities if those opportunities cannot be seized."[17] With the question posed in these epic terms, and in a speech at Fulton that had been set up in a way that guaranteed the attention of the world's press, it is not surprising that reactions were strong. The myth that almost everyone in the United States was hostile to the Fulton speech and saw the light only later was long ago demolished by Fraser Harbutt. Taken as a whole, opinion was fairly evenly divided, but with regional concentrations of support in the press on the East and West Coasts and with the main area of hostility in the traditionally isolationist Midwest. Even to that pattern there were significant exceptions, for William Allen White, editor of the influential *Emporia Gazette* in Kansas, was one of the first to rally to

15. Speech notes, House of Commons, Dec. 13, 1945, CP 5/2; Speech notes, Miami, Feb. 26, 1946, CP 5/4.
16. Account of Clark Clifford, Truman's counsel, quoted in *WSC* VIII 196. The story is broadly confirmed by Charles Ross, Truman's press secretary, and another of the poker players of 1946 (Charles Ross Diary, Harry S. Truman Presidential Library).
17. Churchill to Truman, Nov. 29, 1945, CP 2/230.

Churchill, telling him that if his speech "fail[ed] to pull the democratic world together to meet the crisis, I don't think that anything else can succeed."[18]

What cannot be denied, though, is the violence of feeling on both sides in the few days after the speech was delivered. As he prepared for his speech in New York on March 15, Churchill was deluged with telegrams that variously urged him to go home, to stop talking about freedom and democracy at least until Britain got out of Ireland, or conversely to stick in there and keep pitching. A Baptist clergyman cabled: "Ignore the boos. They're all dirty rats. Pull no punches," and a golf club president from Brooklyn chimed in with "Attaboy Winnie, give Uncle Joe the needle. 100 million behind you," while "a disabled veteran" asked, "Don't you believe you have caused enough trouble? It's time you went back to your island." The British consul general in New York had the thousand or so letters and telegrams sent to Churchill analyzed and found that only about 18 percent were actually hostile, and that these tended to show "a marked similarity of wording [that] made the sudden spate of abuse seem anything but spontaneous." It was noticeable, though, that hardly any of the thousand letters were in any way neutral or borderline—all came down for or against. And since some of those that were against came down very hard indeed, it is unsurprising that the administration took the opportunity to deny its involvement, stand back, and await the firming up of opinion. For example, the National Maritime Union, exactly the type of blue-collar group on which Truman's Democrats relied for support, expressed trenchant views:

> The Tory wail of Winston Churchill to the American youth
> of Westminster College in your native state is repugnant and

18. Harbutt, "The Fulton Speech and the Iran Crisis of 1946," Ph.D. thesis, University of California at Berkeley, 1979; see also summaries of radio commentaries and press reactions sent to Churchill from the White House press office, Mar. 7, 1946, CP 2/29; W. A. White to Churchill, Mar. 9, 1946, CP 2/230. Harbutt argues that the readiness of most Americans to accept from Churchill that there was a problem in respect of the Soviet Union that had to be addressed meant that even those who initially rejected his prescription of an alliance were eventually drawn into that too, because there was no other policy to deal with the problem that they now acknowledged, a device that owed something to the cunning with which Churchill had made his two major propositions at Fulton (without ever formally linking them), but that was not spotted by the opponents of the speech until too late (*Iron Curtain*, 203).

insulting. . . . Loyal Americans [are] aghast at the crass impu-
dence and lack of respect evidenced by a subject of another nation over-enjoying our hospitality. . . . We cannot believe that you
willingly or knowingly lent aid and comfort or accepted his proposal to save the crumbling Empire at the cost of one American
boy's life.[19]

Whatever else he had done, Churchill had certainly got his proposals
into the debate.[20]

## *The View from London — and Ottawa*

None of this could have happened without at least the acquiescence
of the British government, but in some areas it was a case more of active support than of acquiescence. British diplomats in the United
States treated Churchill more like a visiting premier than a private
citizen, and thus undoubtedly contributed to the impression of
many Americans that his was, despite all the disclaimers, an official
visit on behalf of the government. Churchill was in any case fond of
emphasizing the continuity of British policy since Anthony Eden had
been replaced at the foreign office, something that neatly obscured
the gap between government and Opposition. The British Information Service in New York sent to Churchill in Miami copies of all the
BBC's news bulletins and regular digests of the London press; the
British consul general in New York looked after "the details of Mr.
Churchill's schedule there and [was] responsible for providing trans-
portation etc."; British consuls in Miami and New York dealt with
all the casual letters written to Churchill by ordinary Americans —
almost two thousand letters in Florida alone (three hundred of
which included such gifts as cigars, brandy, and sides of ham) —
sorted them, analyzed them, and presumably answered them, too;

19. These telegrams and many others are filed in CP 2/226. Mail analysis from
consul general, Mar. 27, 1946, CP 2/229; National Maritime Union to Truman,
copied to Churchill, Mar. 17, 1946, CP 2/226.
20. The most imaginative response in a critical tone came from the American
communists, who declared that the sun never set on the British Empire because God
did not trust Winston Churchill in the dark, a joke that so amused Churchill that he
insisted on hearing it again (Pilpel, *Churchill in America*, 228).

the foreign-office bag was made available for Churchill's correspondence with his party colleagues in London, and when a cable went astray it was the British ambassador who received the complaint rather than the cable company.[21] Churchill seems indeed to have taken such support as his right in 1946; he wrote to Lord Halifax that he would expect him to "shelter" him while he was in Washington. Although the foreign-office bag was supposed to be only for "important communications," he used it among other things to send his French watch back to Paris for repair. And he seems to have felt no great obligation to be helpful in return; when the Washington embassy asked Churchill to give some time to a visit from a congressman who had been "of great help to the British authorities in connection with the British economic situation after the War and with the loan," the telegram was unceremoniously marked "No" by Churchill himself, and no interview was granted.[22]

But British government help went further than administrative and logistic support, for without the government's approval of the trip, Churchill could never have crossed the Atlantic in the first place. Shipping and air transport were still rigorously controlled in the winter of 1945–1946, and Churchill had to assure the minister of war transport that his visit had been cleared with the prime minister and the foreign secretary before he was able to secure berths for his large party on board the *Queen Elizabeth*. In case this seems no more than a technical matter—the application to Churchill of general regulations that were not meant to apply to persons such as himself—another piece of transatlantic business needs to be considered. As a consequence of his American trip, Churchill was asked to send a contribution to a fund to restore the Jerome family church, but his request to the cabinet office to allow him to send the scarcely extravagant sum of twenty-five pounds to this good cause was sternly rejected, by a civil servant in the first instance and by Hugh Dalton

21. Churchill's secretary to Charles Campbell, Jan. 24, 1946, CP 2/224; Miss Sturdee to Philip Hayden, Columbia University, Feb. 22, 1946, CP 2/225; mail analysis by British consul, Miami, Mar. 12, 1946, CP 2/228; note on New York mail by British consul general, Mar. 27, 1946, CP 2/229; note on logistic arrangements for trip, Jan. 10, 1946, CP 2/229; and see Harbutt, *Iron Curtain*, 227.
22. Churchill to Halifax, Dec. 9, 1945, CP 2/227; Churchill to Duff Cooper, Apr. 7, 1946, CP 2/5; Washington embassy to Churchill, Feb. 18, 1946, CP 2/225.

when Churchill appealed to the chancellor, even though Churchill reminded them that his "family association with the United States has been of public advantage during the War and might still be of public advantage." No exceptions could be made to the policy of exchange control, even for Churchill; in response he thundered that he did not consider that "this particular exercise of arbitrary power is an instance of wise or sensible judgment." But when he decided instead to send the Jeromes a dozen signed photographs that could be raffled in New York (which presumably raised far more than twenty-five pounds), he found that he had to apply for a special export license. It is then quite clear that the British government could easily have obstructed Churchill's American visit in 1946.[23]

It was, of course, highly unlikely that they would, for in many and various ways a Churchill visit would be helpful to Britain's interests in North America, whatever he actually said in the big speech. Sarah Oliver told her father when the trip was over that he had "contributed much to the world cause, quite apart from what you did for poor old England," and the diplomats seem to have agreed; the British consul based in Baltimore reported that Churchill's visit to Virginia had done "more in twenty-four hours to help us than we could have accomplished in months."[24] In part this was a matter of putting him on display so that he could meet many prominent Americans, and of the private meetings with the more famous that the embassy was able to schedule, such as Governor Thomas Dewey. In part it was simply that for Americans who were pro-British, Churchill in their midst was a reminder of all that he had symbolized since 1940; one Miami pressman, who heard only an impromptu Churchill address from the balcony of the yacht club, nevertheless found that Churchill's voice revived his admiration for "Old England, which has always held aloft the banner of freedom.... It re-lit memories of those dark days when, huddled with others about a radio in a small United States village, I heard, 'We shall fight them on the beaches....'" Churchill understood well the impact that his

23. Churchill to Alfred Barnes, Dec. 14, 1946, CP 2/228; Miss Gillette to Burke Trend, Dec. 3, 1946, and attached correspondence, CP 1/41; *WSC* VIII 173–74.
24. Sarah Oliver to Churchill, Apr. 1, 1946, CP 1/41; Harold Braham to Churchill, Mar. 12, 1946, CP 2/224.

established reputation could now have on American opinion. As he told Attlee a few weeks later, when seeking permission to use cabinet documents in his forthcoming war memoirs: "I think [the war memoirs] could win sympathy for our country, particularly in the United States, and make them understand the awful character of the trials through which we passed, especially when we were fighting alone, and the moral debt owed to us by other countries."[25] American critics of Churchill's speech at Fulton were also aware of this, for many of them complained precisely about Churchill using his hold over American opinion to influence future policy; one telegram argued to Truman that "British expectations as exposed by Churchill for eternal lend-lease is only typical," and another urged Churchill to "go home and quit begging for more dollars." The sort of reaction to Churchill that such people feared was typified by the southerner who wired: "Just heard your speech. You talk like a Texan, you act like a Texan, and God bless you. And we are with you for all the English-Speaking peoples."[26] At a time during which the foreign secretary was desperate to keep American troops in Europe, such sentiments could only be helpful to Britain's case.

Beyond this general advantage to Britain from Churchill's visit, it can be argued that Attlee's ministers had nothing much to lose from encouraging it to take place. Responsibility for a Conservative politician's speech was much more deniable for a Labour prime minister thousands of miles away than it was for the American president who had arranged it and witnessed it in person, and while the American press scarcely treated Truman's denial of foreknowledge as remotely credible, the British press showed no equivalent skepticism about Attlee and Bevin. The Labour government could therefore benefit from the military and diplomatic consequences of what Churchill had said while continuing to proclaim the unlimited goodwill toward Stalin that the Labour Party wanted to hear. Almost a year after the Fulton speech, "Cassandra" was still telling his *Sunday Pictorial* readers that

25. Halifax to Churchill, Mar. 7, 1946, CP 2/225; Philip C. Clarke to Churchill, Feb. 4, 1946, CP 2/224; Churchill to Attlee, May 29, 1946, CP 2/4.

26. National Maritime Union to President Truman, Mar. 17, 1946, J. E. Mason to Churchill, Mar. 16, 1946, and "A Texan," Ned Tankersley, to Churchill, Mar. 15, 1946, CP 2/226.

Ernest Bevin's main foreign policy aim was to improve relations with Russia, and denouncing in the process Randolph Churchill's recent "incendiary" lectures in the United States as even more irresponsible than his father's had been.[27]

But did the British government have foreknowledge of what Churchill was to say at Fulton, and was their denial of responsibility therefore disingenuous? Churchill told Lord Halifax, British ambassador in Washington, that he had only accepted the invitation to Fulton to talk about "foreign affairs" after the foreign office had indicated that it would be "agreeable to them," and he told War Transport Minister Alfred Barnes that he had "made the Foreign Secretary and the Prime Minister acquainted with this project of mine some time ago, and have been informed by them that, as far as they are concerned in the matter, they view my movements with approval."[28] Although Churchill reported the same conversations to Truman rather more positively—saying that Attlee viewed his visit "with favour"—the wording of his letter to Barnes (who was likely to check with Attlee, and would therefore have to be told the truth) suggests something less than close involvement. There is no evidence of much further contact on the subject between Churchill and the British government until the actual speech, though the report that Churchill sent Attlee on February 21 was positively misleading, indicating only that he was likely to speak along the lines of his Harvard speech of 1943, which had been for closer Anglo-American relations

---

27. *Sunday Pictorial*, Jan. 26, 1947; Randolph Churchill was, said "Cassandra," "explaining to the American people the details which his father carefully omitted to supply when he made the Fulton speech. What Winston Churchill considered to be too inflammable to explain at length, his incendiary son ignites with . . . reckless gusto." This was unfair, for Randolph was (for once) trying to remain entirely within Churchill's careful bounds; he reminded American listeners to his *Europe Today* broadcast on CBS that Churchill had not called for a military alliance at Fulton but for a fraternal understanding such as the United States already had with Canada, and that Churchill's "so-called 'denunciation' of Russia" at Fulton had been "mild and restrained" when compared with what had been heard since from "responsible government spokesmen, like Mr. Byrnes, Mr. Bevin and Mr. Attlee." The problem with the Fulton speech, thought Randolph, lay not in its content, but in the "re-write men and headline writers" who had inaccurately summarized it and sensationalized its message (transcript of broadcast enclosed with Randolph Churchill to Winston Churchill, Nov. 2, 1946, CP 1/41).

28. Churchill to Halifax, Dec. 9, 1945, CP 2/227; Churchill to Alfred Barnes, Dec. 14, 1946, CP 2/228.

without being against Russia; this shows among other things that
Churchill and Truman had also agreed in advance on the smoke
screen that they would use to deflect interference. Churchill eventually sent to Attlee and Bevin a full account of what he had said, why
he had said it, and how in his opinion all of this fitted into developing American administration attitudes to Russia, but not until March
7. This six-hundred-word cable produced after a week's delay a char-
acteristically laconic response from Attlee, expressing thanks for
Churchill's "long and interesting telegram" but making no comment whatsoever on anything that Churchill had said either at Fulton or in his telegram.[29]

The British embassy in Washington could not take so distanced a
view, and the fact that it was headed until May 1946 by Churchill's
appointee and former Tory colleague Lord Halifax made detachment
from Churchill's "project" even more unlikely. Halifax wrote to welcome Churchill's American visit with the partisan reminder that
"your American friends…are still frankly puzzled at what seemed to
them the great ingratitude of the British people."[30] Once Churchill
was in America, Halifax not only helped make the arrangements but
also told him what he should say in his speeches. Before the Fulton
speech, Halifax suggested ways in which the coming speech could be
made amenable to American opinion, and endured Churchill trying
a good deal of it out on him as an audience, "with tears almost
rolling down his cheeks as he thought of the great strategical concept of the future." After Fulton, when Churchill was preparing his
New York speech, Halifax sent a far more detailed set of recommendations. First, he depreciated "U[ncle] J[oe]'s speech" as "pretty in-
solent, but I suppose he would say that you began it. Any public

29. Churchill to Truman, Nov. 8, 1945, Harry S. Truman Presidential Papers,
General File GF 115, "Churchill, Winston," Harry S. Truman Presidential Library;
Harbutt, *Iron Curtain,* 171; Churchill to Attlee, Mar. 7, 1946, and Attlee to
Churchill, Mar. 14, 1946, CP 2/4.
30. Halifax to Churchill, Dec. 3, 1945, CP 2/227. Despite earlier conflicts and
Halifax's recent irritation with Churchill when he refused to vote in the Commons in
December 1945 to approve the American loan on which he had expended such ef-
fort, Halifax and Churchill remained on good terms; Churchill wanted Halifax back
in his shadow cabinet as soon as he returned from Washington, and Halifax resisted
this only on the grounds that he could not take a partisan line so soon after being
Labour's ambassador.

argument between you will get the world nowhere except into a worse temper." He therefore suggested that Churchill explain that Stalin had misunderstood what he had said at Fulton, but argue also that Stalin "does not appear to appreciate any of the causes that are responsible for the present anxiety about Russian policy"; Churchill should pay a warm tribute to Russian sacrifices during the war and refuse to allow Anglo-Russian friendship "to be frosted over," and he should therefore offer to travel from America to Moscow for "a full and frank discussion" of world affairs with Stalin. Halifax believed "that something of this kind would have a profound effect both in the United States and at home, and that it might do something that neither Attlee nor Truman could do." If Churchill were to accept the idea of personal diplomacy in Moscow, Halifax volunteered to recommend the idea to the British government on his own behalf.[31]

Churchill's New York speech followed these prescriptions fairly closely. Surprisingly—in view of his faith in personal diplomacy, his conviction that he alone among Western statesmen could handle Stalin, and his later adoption of just such a summit-meeting strategy for winding down the cold war in 1950—he did not suggest a trip to Moscow, but all of Halifax's other suggestions found their way into the speech, and the ambassador was accordingly enthusiastic about what Churchill said to the New Yorkers: he cabled his "warmest congratulations on your last night's speech.... Dorothy and I listened in and I felt much better for it."[32] Halifax was pursuing a personal line here, having failed in a devious attempt to get his foreign secretary to come into line with the new anti-Soviet policy in advance, though without briefing him on Churchill's intentions. Although he was coming adrift from his own government, Halifax kept in step with the American administration; his need to consult may explain why it took nine of the ten days that passed between Churchill's Fulton and New York speeches before Halifax made his proposals by urgent telegram, and why the idea of a trip to Moscow had a curious similarity to Truman's own reaction to Stalin's denunciation of Churchill, which was

31. Halifax to Churchill, Feb. 8, 1946, CP 2/227; Halifax diary quoted in Harbutt, *Iron Curtain*, 162; Halifax to Churchill, Mar. 14, 1946, CP 2/6.
32. Halifax to Churchill, Mar. 16, 1946, CP 2/26.

to invite the Russian leader to come to Missouri and make a speech of his own at Columbia.[33]

In public in any case, Attlee and Bevin kept their distance, and it was reported all across the world that "official sources" in London had denied that Churchill "had the approval of the British Government." That view was maintained even when Churchill himself sought advice; when he received the congratulations of the Brazilian Christian Democratic Party on his American speeches, the foreign office suggested that "in view of the somewhat controversial nature of the message, we feel that it would be wiser to send no acknowledgment." Nevertheless, despite the need of the Labour government to keep its own left-wingers happy, in the cabinet as well as in the Commons, it was by then receiving hawkish advice from its own ambassador in Moscow, Frank Roberts, in a tone remarkably similar to what George Kennan was sending back to Washington, and foreign-office analyses of the Russian press indicated a breakdown of Russo-American relations on both sides. These were developments that Bevin could hardly ignore, and if he was not going to be trapped into giving public support for Churchill, neither was he going to be cornered into repudiating him.[34]

A second channel of communication relates to Canada, for Mackenzie King in Ottawa (at that stage moving rapidly into an anti-communist mood as the trial of Russian spies threatened his government) was also involved actively in forwarding Churchill's "project," having agreed with Churchill's objective of bringing the United States and the British Commonwealth closer together in London in the previous November. In advance of Churchill's speech at Fulton, King sent him a copy of the Ogdensburg agreement of August 1940,

33. Truman's offer to bring Stalin to the United States on the USS *Missouri* hardly made the Russian leader's acceptance likely (Harbutt, *Iron Curtain*, 171–72; David McCullough, *Truman* [New York: Simon and Schuster, 1992], 490).

34. *Ottawa Journal*, Mar. 5, 1946; J. N. Henderson to Churchill, Apr. 11, 1946, CP 2/5; Walker, *Cold War*, 43; Alan Bullock, *Ernest Bevin, Foreign Secretary, 1945–1951* (London: Heinemann, 1983), 222, 225–26; John Charmley, *Churchill's Grand Alliance* (London: Hodder and Stoughton, 1995), 226. Attlee certainly claimed not to know in advance of Churchill's intentions, and to have been worried that the Fulton speech would in fact be counterproductive by antagonizing Americans, until Churchill's own assurance that he had Truman's backing reassured him (Francis Williams, ed., *A Prime Minister Remembers* [London: Heinemann, 1961], 162).

by which Canada and the United States set up their joint board of defense, "which may be of some use in connection with your forthcoming address." This suggests at the least some detailed foreknowledge of what Churchill was going to say, probably from Churchill's discussions with the Canadian ambassador during his trip to Washington. On the day after Fulton, King not only sent Churchill "heartiest congratulations on what I believe is already generally regarded as the greatest and most significant of your many epoch-making public addresses," but he also cabled Attlee that the Fulton speech was "the most courageous utterance that I have ever heard from a public man," helpfully sending a copy of this cable to Churchill. When Churchill was criticized after Fulton, King wrote again, urging him, like Halifax, to stress in his New York speech the idea of practical cooperation rather than a binding alliance, for "I can see no justification whatever for an attack being made on the extension of what is already in existence and warmly approved by the United States." When Churchill in New York followed his advice— or at least spoke along the same lines—King was even more jubilant: "What you said," he cabled Churchill, "seemed to me, in the light of the discussion which has taken place since your address at Fulton, to be just what was needed in the way of supplement."[35]

It seems unlikely that the foreign office was unaware of these attempts to get Churchill at least to modify what he had said at Fulton, even if they had no foreknowledge of the original speech, and there remains at least the suspicion that the British government felt they were too close for comfort to Churchill during his American trip. Although Churchill and Bevin remained on friendly terms after the former's return to London, and agreed without difficulty not only on the timing of foreign-policy debates but also on which issues should and should not be raised, the government nevertheless resisted Churchill's demands that he continue to be briefed at a high level on international developments and nuclear policy. Churchill became increasingly irritated by this and eventually complained to Attlee,

35. *WSC* VIII 162; King to Churchill, Mar. 1, 1946, CP 2/7; Harbutt, *Iron Curtain*, 162; King to Churchill, Mar. 6, 1946, CP 2/228; King to Churchill, Mar. 14, 1946 (enclosing King to Attlee, Mar. 5, 1946), and King to Churchill, Mar. 16, 1946, CP 2/7.

reminding him that he had generously taken Attlee to Potsdam with him in 1945. Attlee's reply, a classic "Clem" put-down, among other things reminded Churchill that Britain had been in the midst of a general election in June 1945, an election that Churchill had called against Labour advice, and pointed out that as Labour's leader from 1935 onward he knew all the precedents, so he could tell Churchill just how little his Tory predecessors had involved the Opposition in the making of policy. But Attlee's letter also included a paragraph that unmistakably referred back to Fulton: "You are, I am sure, aware of the tendency of certain Foreign Powers to believe that speeches by eminent persons like yourself, must have been concerted with the Government. This has been an embarrassment to us, and doubtless to you." If Churchill were indeed to remain briefed much like a minister, Attlee felt, then it would impose restraints on him of the type that an Opposition leader ought not to have to face. That last point was prophetic, for when in 1949 Attlee briefed Churchill and other senior Conservatives on Privy Council terms, on details of defense policy, it was eventually Churchill who broke off the talks because inside knowledge to which he could not refer in public did indeed inhibit his position as Opposition leader.[36]

Curiously, the people who remained most in the dark about Churchill's activities in America were not the Labour government but the Conservative Opposition. Deputy Leader Eden certainly did not know in advance what Churchill was going to say, and had difficulty fielding journalists' questions about the speech, both before it was delivered and afterward; paradoxically, it was Attlee rather than Churchill who provided Eden with a copy of Churchill's telegram explaining what he was up to. Privately, Eden deplored Churchill's increasingly anti-Russian rhetoric, and even told a friend that he sometimes suspected Churchill of trying to start another war simply

36. Churchill to Eden, enclosing correspondence with Bevin, Apr. 12, 1946, CP 2/5; Attlee to Churchill, Oct. 9, 1946, CP 2/4. Attlee's claim that Stalin saw Churchill as a representative of the British government was borne out by a conversation that the British ambassador had with Stalin in May: he reported that "When I insisted that Mr. Churchill had spoken as a private individual," Stalin replied, "There are no such private individuals in this country" (quoted in Harbutt, *Iron Curtain*, 211; John Ramsden, *The Age of Churchill and Eden, 1940–1957* [London: Longman, 1995], 196).

to get himself back into office. But Eden was out of line in a party that had never much liked the Russian alliance and was now most unlikely to condemn its leader for being too anticommunist. Duff Cooper reassured Churchill that his speech had been "well-received in Conservative circles," and the shadow cabinet had the Conservative chief whip cable their leader with their "sincere congratulations on a magnificent speech." This was the telegram that went astray, and Churchill's reaction when it eventually came to light indicates his uncertainty as to how even his supporters would react to Fulton: "I should have been much comforted to have had it at the time." Although British Conservative politicians overwhelmingly backed what Churchill had said, this was less true of the Tory press; only the *Daily Telegraph* and the *Daily Mail* backed Churchill unreservedly, while the *Times* thought his words inflammatory and the *Daily Express* remained committed more to British imperialism than to a special relationship with the United States. This cannot have helped Churchill's confidence, for the *Times* and the *Express* (together with the equally hostile, left-inclined *Daily Mirror*) were the only British papers that he had arranged to have sent to him in America on a daily basis.[37]

## *"Truman Didn't Know"—or Did He?*

When we move to the question of the American administration's involvement, the issues become clearer. Most obviously, Truman pulled out all the stops to ensure that Churchill had an enjoyable trip. His personal pilot carried messages for Churchill, he sent his own aircraft to ferry Churchill to Cuba and back, and later to Washington, and he would have provided a USAAF plane for prospective visits to Trinidad and Brazil had Churchill's health not prevented these additional forays. Truman seems to have assisted with the provision of a brand-new Cadillac and chauffeur that were at Churchill's disposal during his two months in the United States, he was ready to

37. David Dutton, *Anthony Eden* (London: Arnold, 1997), 319–20; Duff Cooper to Churchill, Apr. 2, 1946, CP 2/5; James Stuart to Churchill, Mar. 7, 1946, and Churchill to Halifax, Apr. 10, 1946, CP 2/6; C. J. Bartlett, *The Special Relationship* (London: Longman, 1992), 22.

entertain the whole Churchill party on his presidential yacht off the Florida coast as well as at the White House, and he intervened personally to ensure that the authorities in New York left the exhausted Churchill alone when he first arrived. His staff made the arrangements for the visit to Missouri, and Mrs. Churchill stayed at the White House while her husband and the president were in the Midwest, so saving her the fatigue of the journey. When Churchill at the last moment changed his mind and asked if he and Truman could travel to Missouri by train rather than by air, the president rearranged his schedule at a fortnight's notice and committed two additional days to getting to Missouri and back. This last point suggests that presidential support went well beyond the good manners expected even of a host with a distinguished guest.[38]

The change from airplane to a convivial all-male party that would spend three days together on a long-distance train journey did, however, make a social difference of the first order; and several of the participants had vivid recollections of Churchill's "zippered black-out suit," his high spirits (particularly after the speech had been delivered), his inability to grasp the rules of poker, and that "he and the President got on famously," as press secretary Charles Ross put it. Over several games of late-night poker—during which the president first told his card-playing staffers that they must not be seen to allow Churchill to win, but later reversed the advice when Churchill's losses mounted alarmingly—Churchill and Truman became good friends rather than just political allies: "If I am going to play poker with you, Mr. President," declared Churchill, "I am going to call you Harry," to which Truman replied, "All right, Winston." This became a permanent rather than a temporary change of protocol; Churchill's letter to Truman after Fulton began with the words, "My dear Harry (you see I am obeying your commands)," and was accompanied by signed sets of Churchill's war speeches and of his Marlborough biography as a further sign of personal goodwill. An indication of how close the relationship became is to be found in badinage recorded during that famous

38. Churchill to Truman, Jan. 29, 1946, CP 2/158; General Eaker to Churchill, Jan. 28, 1946, CP 2/226; Churchill to General Motors, Jan. 25, 1946, and Churchill to Col. Clarke, Dec. 10, 1945, CP 2/225; Churchill to Truman, Feb. 14, 1946, CP 2/158; schedule for train journey, Mar. 4–7, 1946, CP 2/230.

train ride; on one occasion Churchill explained that he had only one complaint to make about Americans, which was that they stopped drinking during mealtimes, and when Truman rejoined that the custom was just dandy since it allowed Americans to save enough money on wines and spirits to bail out Great Britain with postwar loans, Churchill countered that "the great American pastime these days seems to be twisting the loan's tail."[39]

Thereafter, Truman was on the list of those who routinely received birthday and Christmas messages and complimentary copies of each Churchill book, and throughout their later correspondence and meetings there were almost obligatory references back to the trip to Missouri in March 1946. They discovered that they had things in common over and above politics; for example, both had a daughter in the arts of whom they were each inordinately proud. When Truman discovered that Sarah Oliver was appearing in a play in Maryland in 1949, he took a full presidential party from Washington to see her, and was photographed with the cast. Churchill duly received prints, and Truman later also sent photo-graphs showing their two daughters together when they met in Atlanta, gestures that were warmly appreciated by the always family-conscious Churchill.[40] Churchill's precarious health and the danger that bad weather conditions would prevent them from getting to Missouri at all if they relied on air transport, the reasons given by Churchill for preferring a train ride, were reasonable, but in view of Churchill's known preference for personal contacts it seems at least plausible that he was also motivated by the desire to get Truman to himself for a few days, aiming at exactly the result that he got. The unbuttoned atmosphere of the train journey encouraged the Americans to tell Churchill things about their developing policy that he had not discovered in earlier formal meetings, and so to judge more precisely the impact that his speech would make. And it was still not too late, for final adjustments to the text were made during the train journey, and a final version typed up only at the last minute; the most famous paragraph in the speech, referring to the "iron curtain,"

39. Diary of Charles Ross, Mar. 7, 1946, Harry S. Truman Presidential Library; Churchill to Truman, Mar. 7, 1946, CP 2/158; Pilpel, *Churchill in America*, 218.
40. Truman to Churchill, Sept. 27, 1949, CP 2/158.

seems to have appeared only at that late stage, within a few hours of the speech's delivery.[41]

Perhaps the best way to analyze the evidence is as a convergence of views between Churchill and Truman that began even in the autumn of 1945, when the Missouri visit was being arranged. The story began with Truman's Navy Day speech, delivered on October 27, generally regarded as his first shot across Stalin's bows, the first hint of a tougher American policy to come. Churchill received a copy of Truman's speech when he was preparing his first speech on foreign policy since he had ceased to be prime minister, for a Commons debate on November 7. In that speech he described what Truman had said as "momentous," and he urged the Commons to concentrate on Anglo-American relations as "the supreme matter." He returned to Truman's speech later in his own remarks, summarized what Truman had said as committing the United States to defend democracy even at the risk of war (which was actually rather further than Truman had gone), and warmly endorsed Truman's approach. The next day, Churchill wrote to Truman to accept his invitation to Fulton, which had been sent to him a couple of weeks earlier (in other words, while Truman had been preparing *his* speech): "I dare say you will have seen from the speech I made yesterday," wrote Churchill, "how very much I admire your recent declarations and my great desire to carry forward the policy which you announced by every means in the power of the Conservative Party." Interestingly too, in the context of possible British foreknowledge of Churchill's Fulton speech, that letter from Churchill to Truman was hand delivered by Attlee's secretary, Leslie Rowan, who was accompanying Attlee to meet Truman in Canada. It seems inconceivable that Attlee would not already have grasped the turn of events in November 1945, five months before Fulton. When they met at the White House in February, the diary of Truman's chief of staff demonstrates

---

41. Speech notes, Fulton, Mar. 5, 1946, CP 5/4. The idea that the "iron curtain" paragraph was added at the last minute has been popularly believed for years, but is impossible to prove from the speech file in the Churchill Papers. It is given some credibility, though, from the fact that the paragraph was on its own (incomplete) page in the press release, and was not included in advance copies issued to the eastern press before Churchill left Washington. Some eastern papers did not therefore include any reference to the speech's most famous passage in their first reports.

just how close their views had become in private, and Fraser Harbutt has indeed argued that it was during the couple of days during which Churchill was with Truman in mid-February that American policy toward Russia actually changed. By early March, convergence had become public, and, reflecting on his Fulton speech in his telegram to Attlee, Churchill concluded:

> Having spent nearly three days in most intimate, friendly contact with the President and his immediate circle, and also having had a long talk with Mr. Byrnes, I have no doubt that the Executive forces here are deeply distressed at the way they are being treated by Russia, and that they do not intend to put up with treaty breaches in Persia or encroachments in Manchuria and Korea, or pressure from the Russian expansion at the expense of Turkey in the Mediterranean. I am convinced that some show of strength and resisting power is necessary to a good settlement with Russia. I predict that this will be the prevailing opinion in the United States in the near future.[42]

Churchill's own views, his assessment of U.S. government opinion, and his prediction of future events after Fulton were by then all in step.

How much, though, was this an implicit convergence, and how much was the speech actually the result of collusion with American officials? Despite the repeated denials—which, as a New York paper remarked, had convinced nobody—it is clear that the Truman administration knew in advance exactly what Churchill meant to say at Fulton, and thoroughly approved of it in private, even while denying its complicity in public. As far back as November 1945, Churchill had assured Truman: "Naturally I would let you know beforehand the line which I propose to take...so that nothing should be said by me on this occasion which would cause you embarrassment. I do not however think this likely to happen, as we are so much agreed in our general outlook." On January 29, soon after arriving in America, Churchill reminded Truman: "I need a talk with you about our Fulton date. I have a message...and I think it very likely that we shall be in full agreement about it." During February, Churchill flew to Washington to meet Truman and other members of the administration,

---

42. Speech notes and preparatory papers, House of Commons, Nov. 7, 1945, CP 5/2; Churchill to Truman, Nov. 8, 1945, CP 2/4; Harbutt, *Iron Curtain*, 161; Churchill to Attlee, Mar. 7, 1946, CP 2/4.

and Secretary of State Byrnes flew to Miami for further discussions with Churchill. Truman also received from the American ambassador in Cuba a detailed account of a dinner conversation with Churchill in which he had outlined his views in full, which told Truman almost everything that would be coming at Fulton even if he had had no other sources. In respect of the speech text itself, Churchill reported to Attlee that he had first showed it to Admiral Leahy, Truman's chief of staff, who "was enthusiastic"; on the evening before boarding the train, he showed the latest draft to Secretary Byrnes, who "was excited about it and did not suggest any alterations." Finally, during the train journey, Churchill showed the text to Truman himself, who "told me he thought it was admirable and would do nothing but good, though it would make a stir. He seemed equally pleased during and after" the speech's delivery. It was only because Truman had been careful to read "a mimeographed reproduction," rather than "the exact text" from which Churchill read, that he could claim that he had not seen "the speech" before it was delivered, but this was a transparent evasion to those who were in the know, and the presidential press secretary was not entirely happy about the regular denials that he was instructed to issue.[43] Even so, some Democratic newspapers apparently went along with the fiction that they were being fed from the White House, and explained (as a March 20 editorial put it in "the old reliable" *Raleigh News and Observer*) that "Truman Didn't Know."

Churchill's declaration to Attlee that "I take complete and sole responsibility for what I said, for I altered nothing as the result of my contacts with those high American authorities," was almost equally disingenuous. There was no need to change the speech when these "high...authorities" agreed with it anyway, but the extent to which he had consulted them in advance surely showed that he would have been prepared to make modifications had they asked him to—which is anyway what he had said privately to Truman all along. It did not

43. Churchill to Truman, Nov. 29, 1945, CP 2/230; Churchill to Truman, Jan. 29, 1946, CP 2/158; Henry Norweb to Truman, Feb. 7, 1946, Harry S. Truman Presidential Papers, General File GF 115, "Churchill, Winston, 1945–1946," Harry S. Truman Presidential Library; Churchill to Attlee, Mar. 7, 1946, CP 2/4; diary of Charles Ross, Mar. 18, 1946, Harry S. Truman Presidential Library.

at all suit Churchill's "project" in America to get out of step with what U.S. officials really thought, though he recognized clearly that he might need to get out of step with what they could yet say in public. As he joked when speaking in Virginia three days after Fulton, he would not touch on foreign policy, for "I might easily, for instance, blurt out a lot of things which people know in their hearts are true but are a bit shy of saying in public. [Laughter.] And this might cause a regular commotion and get you all into trouble." This curious status as the only preacher of a truth that others recognized but dared not own merely increased Churchill's standing among his American admirers, and for some it seemed even to prove his message: a businessman from New York cabled on March 15 to express his support for "someone who has the guts to speak so honestly... while our State Department seems to be following the pattern of Neville Chamberlain. If Joe Stalin can scare members of our State Department away from your [New York] dinner tonight, it shows the extreme need for more blunt speeches."[44] This last jibe was a reference to Under Secretary of State Dean Acheson's hasty cancellation of his attendance at Churchill's New York meeting, for in view of the row going on since Fulton the State Department dared not be seen lending open support to Churchill, a reversal of course of which the Anglophile Acheson was thoroughly ashamed; he went instead to a private lunch to meet Churchill at the embassy and there assured him of his support.[45]

Finally, from this viewpoint, what did the administration say privately about the speech while they were all busily denying foreknowledge and responsibility in public? In almost every case, they expressed unqualified approval, much as Acheson did—in private. The liberal secretary Henry Wallace's confident assertion that "Churchill undoubtedly is not speaking either for the American people or their government" showed only how successful Truman's smoke screen had been. Navy Secretary James Forrestal told Churchill on March 8 that "Averell [Harriman] is back and in good form. I do not think you

44. Speech notes, General Assembly of Virginia, Mar. 8, 1946, CP 5/4; Victor Todd to Churchill, Mar. 15, 1946, CP 222/6.
45. Pilpel, *Churchill in America*, 221; Dean Acheson, *Sketches from Life* (New York: Harpers, 1959), 62.

would find him in any profound disagreement with your observations of last Thursday," which from its tone does not suggest much disagreement by Forrestal either. When Harriman himself wrote on March 19, he was entirely unequivocal in his support for the speeches that Churchill had been making in America. Truman was more cautious than were the more hawkish members of his administration, but close reading of his personal letter thanking Churchill for going to Fulton finds an endorsement all the same. He did not directly refer to the content of the Fulton speech, but the letter concluded, "the people of Missouri were highly pleased with your visit and enjoyed what you had to say." When it is remembered that Truman was hugely proud of his home state and had at one time a notice placed on the presidential desk bearing the words, "I'm from Missouri," the coded message becomes clear: the president was one of those "people of Missouri." It was in any event much nearer the truth than Truman's words used in introducing Churchill to speak at Fulton, when he had declared, "I do not know what Mr. Churchill is going to say."[46]

The administration's public reticence owed much to the violence of the criticism that the Fulton speech initially provoked, but by the time Churchill sailed for home on March 20, the tide had already turned decisively in his favor. The mass of New Yorkers who heard Churchill speak on March 15 thoroughly approved of his message, as he was assured by various observers who went to the event as much to read the reaction as to hear him speak. The consul general's analysis of Churchill's mail also found that the pattern had changed within the fortnight after Fulton: at first almost all were favorable, then there was a surge of (probably organized) hostility, but after the New York speech almost every letter was favorable, which rather confirms the importance of the modifications that Churchill had added there, changes that both reduced the negative reaction and accentuated the positive. Events were, of course, as important as what Churchill said after March 5, but the change of opinions was certainly dramatic: an

46. Harbutt, *Iron Curtain*, 199; James Forrestal to Churchill, Mar. 8, 1946, CP 2/26; Harriman to Churchill, Mar. 19, 1946, CP 2/227; Truman to Churchill, Mar. 12, 1946, CP 2/158. Churchill himself still used code on some occasions, signing confidential telegrams as "Colonel Warden" as in the war years. Truman's notes for Fulton, Mar. 5, 1946, Harry S. Truman Presidential Papers, General File GF 115, "Churchill, Winston, 1945–1946," Harry S. Truman Presidential Library.

opinion poll just after Fulton had found only 18 percent favoring an Anglo-American alliance, while a month later the figure was 85 percent. In a message from John D. Rockefeller on March 19, Churchill could feel that his core message had really got through: "Your various utterances," wrote Rockefeller, "so gracious and kindly and yet always so sincere and challenging, have directed again the attention of America to the great opportunity and the equally great responsibility that rests upon it."[47]

In the middle of April, a month after Churchill returned to London, Halifax wrote: "I am quite sure that there has been a steady movement of understanding what your Fulton speech was about and appreciating it. Many people of a kind I should hardly have expected to take that line have said to me what an immense service you rendered by stating the stark realities, and what an effect that had had upon the thinking and the policy of the Administration. I have very little doubt that it is true." By the following October, Truman could assure Churchill that "your Fulton...speech becomes more nearly a prophecy every day." By then the myth of Churchill's solo effort was so well established that the British ambassador and the American president had both come to believe it.[48]

### *"None but He Could Have Said It"*

How then was it possible for the speech to have such considerable impact? Probably for two main reasons: who Churchill actually was in relation to American opinion, and the extremely fortuitous timing of the speech. Frank Clarke thought that it was "almost incredible that the timing could have been so perfect," for Churchill's speeches (which would have been influential even if a year before the event) had in fact "directed the intense spotlight on the dangerous international situation within less than a month of the crisis." This is persuasive, for early

47. Lewis Brown to Churchill, Mar. 19, 1946, CP 2/224; Max Gordon to Churchill, Mar. 16, 1946, CP 2/226; mail analysis by New York consul general, Mar. 27, 1946, and Rockefeller to Churchill, Mar. 19, 1946, CP 2/229; Harbutt, *Iron Curtain*, 204.
48. Halifax to Churchill, Apr. 15, 1946, CP 2/6; Truman to Churchill, Oct. 14, 1947, CP 2/158.

March was indeed the eye of the storm. On February 28, Secretary Byrnes warned the Russians not to push America too far, but on March 1 the Russians announced that they would not continue their withdrawal from Iran as a treaty of 1942 required, and on the very day of Churchill's speech the United States delivered two stiff notes of protest about Russian policy, in Iran and in Manchuria; the *New York Times* pointed out, "One would have to go far...to find two United States protest notes to one power on two different issues on the same day." Even as Churchill journeyed to Fulton, he was told confidentially that the U.S. administration had decided to send home the body of the recently deceased Turkish ambassador with a full naval escort, including a battleship, two aircraft carriers, and many other warships, the nucleus of what was to be a permanent American military presence in the eastern Mediterranean. This was a key moment in the U.S. deployment to confront Russian expansion, and though the decision was not announced until March 6, Churchill immediately grasped its strategic significance, telling Attlee that it was "a very important act of state and one calculated to make Russia understand that she must come to reasonable terms of discussion with the Western democracies." Nor did timeliness end with the speech at Fulton, for on the eve of Churchill's New York address the U.S. press was reporting that Russian tanks were within twenty miles of Teheran, and even more virulent Russian denunciations of Churchill added again to the impact of Russian policy. After Fulton, Stalin was in a double bind over the growing crisis in Iran, for if he pulled back then Churchill's argument that communists respected only a show of force would be vindicated, whereas if he went forward he would prove Churchill's claim of a growing Russian threat and encourage world opinion to unite against him at the United Nations, as happened at the end of March. His decision first to go ahead and then to climb down was perhaps the ideal one—from Churchill's perspective. As a correspondent told Churchill, "the reaction of the Russians to your Fulton address has done more to make America understand" than anything else. So "ripeness [was] all" in relation to the speech; had it come before the Iran crisis, it is likely that Churchill's message would have been generally disregarded, while, as Churchill himself said only seven months later, "if I were to make that speech at the present time and in the same place, it would attract no particular attention."[49]

Finally, where did Churchill's own status fit in, allowing him to make the most of the opportunity that timing gave him? Before departure, he had told his doctor, "I think I can be of some use over there; they will take things from me." When he had completed the mission, Frank Clarke summarized Churchill's success in much the same terms. The typical American, he wrote, had "eliminated from his mind the possibility of further war," but

> since you sailed it is becoming more and more evident that your warnings have caused a realization in this country that a strong and definite foreign policy is the only "overall strategic concept" —to use your own words—which will offset the same drifting, compromising attitude of laissez faire which led up to Munich and the war with Hitler.... Certainly plain talk was needed. Actually you were the only one to whom this country, and for that matter the democratic peoples of the world, would listen.... You have impressed all freedom-loving people with your honesty of purpose and your knowledge and experience of world affairs, and when you speak and send a warning, they are all forced to look the situation squarely in the face.

Churchill's unique status, deriving from his record in the 1930s and the war years, was thus a key catalyst in persuading Americans to engage with the emerging international situation, and though it clearly emerges from the evidence of the Churchill Papers that the British and American governments were in their different ways each complicit in his Fulton "project," it remains clear that the change in informed opinion across the democratic West, which those governments sought but dared not yet openly demand, owed a great deal to Churchill's personal efforts in March 1946; as Pierson Dixon of the British foreign office put it in his diary on March 6: "I must say Winston's speech echoes the sentiments of all. None but he could have said it."[50]

49. Clarke to Churchill, Apr. 4, 1946, CP 2/225; Churchill to Attlee, Mar. 7, 1946, CP 2/4; Randolph S. Churchill, ed., *The Sinews of Peace: Winston S. Churchill's Post-War Speeches* (London: Cassell, 1948), 93, 226; Harbutt, *Iron Curtain*, 181, 215; Lewis Brown to Churchill, Mar. 19, 1946, CP 2/224. For once Bevin was quite wrong about Churchill, saying of the Fulton speech that Churchill "invariably said the right thing at the wrong time" (Harbutt, *Iron Curtain*, 222).

50. Lord Moran, *Winston Churchill: The Struggle for Survival* (London: Sphere Books, 1968), 332; Clarke to Churchill, Apr. 4, 1946, CP 2/225; Harbutt, *Iron Curtain*, 4; WSC VIII 220.

*Two*

༄ *The Beginning of the Cold War*

PAUL A. RAHE

Mine is a simple, if controversial, claim: that the cold war began in Fulton, Missouri, on March 5, 1946, not before, nor—as is generally thought —well after, but on that date at Westminster College as Winston Churchill delivered his now-famous address "The Sinews of Peace." The speech itself was as important an event as Churchill's famous response in the House of Commons to the Munich Agreement on October 5, 1938.[1] Just as the former shocked and outraged many with its ruthless retelling of naked, ugly truths, so the latter shattered illusions long fondly maintained—above all else, the presumption that our Soviet allies were much preferable to our erstwhile Nazi opponents.

In both speeches Churchill shocked and outraged many, but he did something else as well, something far more significant: in each case, he prepared public opinion for what was to come; he issued a warning; he drew a line in the sand; he indicted a policy that would soon be seen to have failed. What he prophesied on October 5, 1938, came to pass, and he presented himself as a

1. For the text, see Winston S. Churchill, *Complete Speeches, 1897–1963,* ed. Robert Rhodes James, 8 vols. (New York: Chelsea House Publishers, 1974), 6:6004–13, hereinafter cited as *CS;* subsequent references will appear parenthetically in the text.

prophet again on March 5, 1946. "Last time," he told his audience at Westminster College,

> I saw it all coming and I cried aloud to my own fellow-country-men and to the world, but no one paid any attention. Up till the year 1933, or even 1935, Germany might have been saved from the awful fate which has overtaken her and we might all have been spared the miseries Hitler let loose upon mankind. There never was a war in history easier to prevent by timely action than the one which has just desolated such great areas of the globe. It could have been prevented in my belief without the firing of a single shot, and Germany might be powerful, prosperous and honoured to-day; but no one would listen and one by one we were all sucked into the awful whirlpool. We surely...must not let that happen again. (12)

It is hard to imagine a former prime minister, the leader of a party just recently defeated in a landslide, securing such attention. But, in 1946, Winston Churchill was no ordinary man. In Britain, though merely the leader of the Opposition, he towered over the prime minister; and in America, because Franklin Delano Roosevelt had passed from the scene, he towered over the president of the United States. He had earned the right to be listened to; he knew this as well as any man; and he deliberately husbanded his rhetorical resources, waiting for the proper moment, in order to maximize the political impact of his intervention. In 1938, his warning had set limits to Neville Chamberlain's flexibility: as events bore out Churchill's analysis of the consequences of the Munich Agreement, his speech became the standard by which British policy would be judged. The same can be said for the Fulton speech: nothing that Churchill did thereafter, not even as prime minister, was of comparable importance to what he did on March 5, 1946, merely by opening his mouth.

## Decades of Reflection

Behind the Fulton speech lay decades of reflection on three subjects that Churchill brought into focus in his address that day: the geopolitical situation in Europe, the nature of communism, and the need for political solidarity among the English-speaking peoples—

not just in England and in America but in the British Empire as well. Regarding Churchill's geopolitical sensitivity, I need not elaborate: it was his heritage as an Englishman. For centuries, his countrymen had kept a beady eye on the continent of Europe, fearful that its dominance by a single great power would threaten Britain's independence. Churchill's understanding of the geopolitical situation is abundantly evident in *The World Crisis* and in his *Marlborough: His Life and Times.* He had given the matter considerable study.

What needs emphasis here is that Winston Churchill's prescience concerning the danger posed by communism and the Soviet regime was, if anything, more impressive than his prescience concerning National Socialism and Hitler's rule in Germany. As Fraser J. Harbutt has shown in his masterful study *The Iron Curtain: Churchill, America, and the Origins of the Cold War,*[2] upon which I draw throughout this chapter, Churchill was among the earliest and fiercest opponents of the Bolsheviks, and what he had to say on the subject in the last months of the First World War and thereafter makes Ronald Reagan in his presidential years look like a fellow traveler of the communists. Churchill was, of course, willing and even eager to make an alliance with the USSR against Germany in the late 1930s, and he did so with great pleasure and relief in 1941—but this was, as he saw it, a matter of necessity. When Hitler invaded Russia, Churchill told the British people exactly what he thought:

> The Nazi regime is indistinguishable from the worst features of Communism. It is devoid of all theme and principle except appetite and racial domination. It excels all forms of human wickedness in the efficiency of its cruelty and ferocious aggression. No one has been a more consistent opponent of Communism than I have for the last twenty-five years. I will unsay no word that I have spoken about it. But all this fades away before the spectacle that is now unfolding. The past, with its crimes, its follies, and its tragedies, flashes away.... [Hitler's] invasion of Russia is no more than a prelude to an attempted invasion of the British Isles.... The Russian danger is, therefore, our danger,

---

2. Fraser J. Harbutt, *The Iron Curtain: Churchill, America, and the Origins of the Cold War* (New York: Oxford University Press, 1986), hereinafter cited as *IC*; where possible, subsequent references will appear parenthetically in the text.

and the danger of the United States, just as the cause of any Russian fighting for his hearth and home is the cause of free men and free peoples in every quarter of the globe.

To an aide, Churchill added, "If Hitler invaded Hell, I would at least make a favourable reference to the Devil in the House of Commons" (*IC*, 34). Even before the war, in 1937, Churchill was inclined to handle Stalin with kid gloves, damning Trotsky as a fanatic and praising Stalin for his practical bent—for the pragmatism and the flexibility that he hoped to find in the man. Throughout the war, he sought in Stalin those qualities, and he tried to encourage them and to nurture them in the man. He did this because he had to—it would have been criminal to have done otherwise. Churchill in no way sought the conflict that arose in the aftermath of the war.

At the same time, Churchill concerned himself with America. Well before the First World War, he had eliminated the United States from among Britain's potential enemies. In August 1914, he told an American reporter, "If England were to be reduced in this war or another...the burden which we are bearing now would fall on to your shoulders." In February 1917, he asked his fellow M.P.'s to ponder "what a supreme event in human history the entry of the United States into the war would be," and he celebrated the fact that "we have seen the United States drawn, not, as in the Napoleonic Wars, into quarrel with us, but to the very verge of war with those we are blockading." In July 1918, he wrote to a friend, "If all goes well England and the United States may act permanently together" (*IC*, 8–9).

But, of course, things did not go well. In January 1919, in the month in which the Paris Peace Conference opened, Churchill warned that his country and the United States must not "leave" the European "continent in a welter of anarchy" (*IC*, 10). He could not, however, persuade Woodrow Wilson to sustain the effort undertaken against the Soviet regime by the Allies after the Bolsheviks had signed with Germany the Treaty of Brest-Litovsk; and in the aftermath of the peace conference, Wilson himself could not bring his countrymen to live up to the responsibilities toward France in particular and Europe more generally that he had undertaken on their behalf.

The consequences were dire. Georges Clemenceau had agreed that Germany would not be dismembered only on condition that the United States and Britain would commit themselves to a defensive alliance with France. Wilson exacted this crucial concession from France but did not deliver on the promises that he made to this end, and this left France—devastated by a war fought almost entirely on its territory—facing a bitter and angry Germany that was in almost all militarily and economically crucial regards intact. As Churchill put it in November 1919, "the whole shape and character of the peace settlement was determined by American influence.... To carry such a policy *halfway* and to carry it no further, to destroy the old organization without attempting to supply the new, to sweep away the imperial system without setting in its place a League of Nations system, would indeed be an act from which America should recoil." In his judgment all that was required "to squander irretrievably the whole victory" would be that the Ottoman empire would follow Austria-Hungary into dissolution and that France would be abandoned and left to face Germany and Russia alone—which is, of course, exactly what transpired (*IC*, 12).

Nonetheless, Churchill persisted throughout the 1920s and the 1930s in seeing the United States as Britain's natural partner. In 1931, he told an American audience, "The two great opposing forces of the future...would be the English speaking peoples and communism" (*IC*, 17). And, of course, he sounded the same theme vis-à-vis Nazi Germany with ever increasing force after Hitler's rise to power. During the war, especially toward the end, when the time came for the three powers within Churchill's Grand Alliance to sort out a settlement for postwar Europe, he pursued two quite different and ultimately incompatible policies simultaneously. On the one hand, he sought to interest the Americans in containing Soviet ambitions; on the other hand, especially at times when it seemed exceedingly likely that the Americans would repeat their mistake in the days of Woodrow Wilson and abandon Europe after determining the outcome of a great war, Churchill sought an accommodation with Joseph Stalin. In effect, he tried to negotiate for his increasingly weak and vulnerable country the best deal that he could get.

## *Triumph and Tragedy*

There is reason that Churchill named the last volume of his war memoirs *Triumph and Tragedy*. As we know now from the dispatches that he sent and from the records of his private conversations, at the very moment that in public he was celebrating the successful outcome of the war in Europe and the achievements of his Grand Alliance among Great Britain, the Union of Soviet Socialist Republics, and the United States of America, in private he was deeply, profoundly distressed. The nightmare of 1919 was happening again before his eyes: same song, second verse, a whole lot louder, and a whole lot worse. The Americans were preparing to pull out of Europe all but a skeletal force, and the Russians evidently had no intention of abiding by the principles outlined in the Atlantic Charter and elaborated in the Declaration on Liberated Europe agreed upon, at Roosevelt's insistence, at the Yalta Conference in February 1945 by Roosevelt, Churchill, and Stalin and guaranteeing to the liberated peoples "democratic institutions of their own choice" and "free elections" (*IC*, 87).

To grasp the full measure of Churchill's anguish, one need read but one document: a telegram that he dispatched to President Truman, a mere three months after the Yalta Conference, on May 12, 1945—some ten months before the Fulton speech:

> I am profoundly concerned about the European situation. I learn that half the American Air Force in Europe has already begun to move to the Pacific theatre. The newspapers are full of the great movements of the American armies out of Europe. Our armies also are, under previous arrangements, likely to undergo a marked reduction. The Canadian Army will certainly leave. The French are weak and difficult to deal with. Anyone can see that in a very short space of time our armed power on the Continent will have vanished, except for moderate forces to hold down Germany.
>
> 2. Meanwhile what is to happen about Russia? I have always worked for friendship with Russia, but, like you, I feel deep anxiety because of their misinterpretation of the Yalta decisions, their attitude towards Poland, their overwhelming influence in the Balkans, excepting Greece, the difficulties they make about Vienna, the combination of Russian power and the territories under their control or occupied, coupled with the Communist

technique in so many other countries, and above all their power to maintain very large armies in the field for a long time. What will be the position in a year or two, when the British and American Armies have melted and the French has not yet been formed on any major scale, when we may have a handful of divisions, mostly French, and when Russia may choose to keep two or three hundred on active service?

3. An iron curtain is drawn down upon their front. We do not know what is going on behind. There seems little doubt that the whole of the regions east of the line Lübeck-Trieste-Corfu will soon be completely in their hands. To this must be added the further enormous area conquered by the American armies between Eisenach and the Elbe, which will, I suppose, in a few weeks be occupied, when the Americans retreat, by the Russian power. All kinds of arrangements will have to be made by General Eisenhower to prevent another immense flight of the German population westward as this enormous Muscovite advance into the centre of Europe takes place. And then the curtain will descend again to a very large extent, if not entirely. Thus a broad band of many hundreds of miles of Russian-occupied territory will isolate us from Poland.

4. Meanwhile the attention of our peoples will be occupied in inflicting severities upon Germany, which is ruined and prostrate, and it would be open to the Russians in a very short time to advance if they chose to the waters of the North Sea and the Atlantic.

5. Surely it is vital now to come to an understanding with Russia, or see where we are with her, before we weaken our armies mortally or retire to the zones of occupation. This can only be done by a personal meeting. I should be most grateful for your opinion and advice. Of course we may take the view that Russia will behave impeccably, and no doubt that offers the most convenient solution. To sum up, this issue of a settlement with Russia before our strength has gone seems to me to dwarf all others.[3]

The fears that Churchill broached on this occasion were not new. In October 1942, he had told his foreign secretary, Anthony Eden, "It would be a measureless disaster if Russian barbarism overlaid the culture and independence of the ancient states of Europe." In April 1943, he observed that "the overwhelming preponderance of Russia remains the dominant fact of the future" while suggesting that "the

---

3. Winston S. Churchill, *The Second World War*, 6 vols. (Boston: Houghton Mifflin, 1948–1953), 6:572–74.

immense weight of Russia will weigh heavily on the new Europe"
(*IC*, 50).

Nor was this lost on the Americans—oblivious though they may
have seemed at the time. In 1944 at Teheran and in 1945 at Yalta,
Roosevelt sought to mediate between Churchill and Stalin: he deliberately left both with the impression that the United States was as
much at odds with the reactionary British Empire as with the revolutionary Soviet Union, if not more so. Roosevelt's ultimate purpose
remains elusive: he was by temperament a dissembler; in approaching
problems, he preferred indirection. He ran for the presidency in
1932 promising to balance the budget, and he did nothing of the
sort. At Teheran and Yalta, he displayed a measure of indifference regarding Europe that left Churchill fearful that Britain would be left
alone, abandoned, to face the Russian bear. At Teheran, the English
statesman remarked to an aide, "The real problem now is Russia. I
*can't* get the Americans to see it" (*IC*, 54).

Stalin was an exceedingly practical man. During the Anglo-Soviet
negotiations in Moscow in December 1941 and January 1942, he
told Anthony Eden that he preferred to have the terms of the Anglo-
Soviet alliance and the arrangements for postwar Europe spelled out
in detail. "A declaration," he said, "I regard as algebra, but an agreement as practical arithmetic. I do not wish to decry algebra, but I
prefer practical arithmetic" (*IC*, 36). Roosevelt was cut from different cloth. His attitude is perhaps best summed up by a remark that
he made to a friend regarding Stalin. "I think," he observed, "if I
give him everything I possibly can and ask nothing from him in return, noblesse oblige, he won't try to annex anything and will work
with me for a world of democracy and peace" (*IC*, 42). In fact, Roosevelt had a very great liking for algebra. He was willing to concede
to Stalin nearly everything that the latter sought in Europe, but he
demanded something in return: that the Soviet Union enter the war
against Japan and that the USSR join the United Nations. At
Teheran, to Churchill's dismay, he agreed to Stalin's demand that
the Western Allies subordinate their entire military policy to an early
invasion of France with an exclusion of Churchill's "soft underbelly"
policy as a consequence. At Yalta, he acquiesced in Stalin's breaches
of the spirit and letter of all prior agreements regarding Poland and

Eastern Europe—all in pursuit of these ends. The only additional proviso that he attached to their agreements was that the Soviet Union accept the Declaration on Liberated Europe.

The Americans were not blind to the consequences. Charles Bohlen, head of the State Department's Soviet section, summed them up at the time in the following way:

> Germany is to be broken up and kept broken up. The states of eastern, southeastern and central Europe will not be permitted to group themselves into any federations or association. France is to be stripped of her colonies and strategic bases beyond her borders and will not be permitted to maintain any appreciable military establishment. Poland and Italy will remain approximately their present territorial size, but it is doubtful if either will be permitted to maintain any appreciable armed force. The result would be that the Soviet Union would be the only important military and political force on the continent of Europe. The rest of Europe would be reduced to military and political impotence. (*IC*, 60)

It is no wonder that Churchill was left shaken by the event, for, though the English statesman shared Roosevelt's liking for algebra, he was no less addicted to practical arithmetic than Joseph Stalin.

It is easy to see what was involved: both Roosevelt and Churchill were concerned with the postwar settlement. The latter was not averse to larger concerns, but he was chiefly focused on practical arrangements: after all, Europe was in Britain's backyard. Roosevelt's focus was largely domestic: in the sphere of foreign relations, he was inclined to be cautious. He had witnessed the disaster produced by the impolitic Wilson, and he was intent on avoiding a repeat. As a consequence, his chief concern, apart from the as-yet-unsettled conflict in the Pacific, had to do with the United Nations Organization and with American public opinion. He wanted the Russians on the inside, not on the outside, and he wanted the American people to be comfortable with America's international commitment. Power relations in Europe were for him a secondary matter. His focus was the ideological—rather than the practical, political—settlement, and he encouraged James F. Byrnes to present the Yalta agreement to the American public entirely in these terms: as a repudiation of the very notion of spheres of influence (*IC*, 91–95).

This was not quite the folly that it may seem. The Yalta Conference may have sanctioned Soviet hegemony in Eastern Europe, but at the same time it threw an obstacle in its way. The Declaration on Liberated Europe was to be a standard by which the Soviet Union's handling of Eastern Europe was to be judged. It was precisely because Soviet behavior violated the Atlantic Charter and the Declaration on Liberated Europe that Churchill was later able so effectively to shift American public opinion. In a sense, the cold war was implicit in the Yalta agreement: with one hand, Roosevelt gave Eastern Europe to Stalin; with the other, he took it away. He conceded in practical arithmetic what he denied in algebra; and Stalin—the man who believed that the Pope had no divisions—presumed that practical arithmetic matters and that algebra does not. The road from Yalta to Fulton is less crooked than one might imagine.

## The Road to Fulton

It is hard to know what would have transpired had Roosevelt lived: there never was a more slippery president than FDR (I say this with all due respect to the current occupant of the White House), and by means of his contradictory conduct of affairs at Yalta, he had left himself a free hand. In any case, he died, and he was succeeded by a less complex, far more direct, but no less intelligent man. And Churchill did everything in his power to bring home to Truman the dangers to which Roosevelt had seemed utterly insensitive.

With Roosevelt, Churchill had had some success: the American president acquiesced in the British plans to prevent a communist takeover of Greece. With Truman, Churchill had similar success: he was able to rally the American president behind his campaign to prevent Tito of Yugoslavia from unilaterally seizing Italian territory. He failed, however, in persuading Eisenhower to move on Berlin and in convincing the American president to delay the withdrawal of American troops from areas conceded to Russian administration: he failed to persuade the Americans to use their military power as leverage to force Russian compliance with the terms of the agreements that both sides had made. When Churchill lost out to the Labour Party in the middle of the Potsdam Conference, he was upset in more than one way. The one consolation was the appointment of Ernest Bevin as foreign secretary, for, despite the latter's distrust of the Americans and his occasional inclination to suggest that he, as a man of the Left, could easily get on with another man of the Left such as Stalin, Bevin persisted in the path blazed by Churchill.

The simple fact is that Truman took some time in making up his mind. He had not been in Roosevelt's inner circle: he was, for all intents and purposes, outside the loop. He inherited his predecessor's advisers, and his political situation was awkward: he was the comparatively unknown successor of an exceedingly popular and effective president, he had no electoral mandate, and he had to make his way cautiously. In the beginning, he did what was easy: he kept to agreements previously made, he sanctioned the exercise of force to make sure that others who were easily coerced adhered to the agreements as well, and he conducted affairs in the manner of Roosevelt and through the men he had inherited.

In the ten months that passed between Churchill's dispatch of the "iron curtain" telegram and his delivery of the Fulton speech, Truman and his aides worked their way toward the position that Churchill had been enunciating for some time. They found Soviet behavior in Eastern Europe distressing, and they were particularly struck by the Soviet Union's conduct in two particulars: its failure to live up to its treaty obligations and withdraw from northern Iran, and its attempt to force Turkey to give it bases in the Dardanelles, to cede it territory in eastern Anatolia, and to install a pro-Soviet government. What the Russians did not do in Iran and what they tried to do with regard to Turkey were equally indicative of ambitions on their part that extended well outside their natural sphere of influence in Eastern Europe. The situation was rendered more disturbing by the fact that Tito was at the same time sponsoring a communist insurgency in Greece—presumably with Stalin's approval.

In the meantime, Churchill reemerged from the isolation that he had imposed on himself in the wake of his electoral defeat. On August 16, 1945, he told the House of Commons that he was especially concerned about the reports that millions of Germans had been expelled from the territory conceded to Poland. Moreover, he then added:

At the present time—I trust a very fleeting time—"police governments" rule over a great number of countries. It is a case of the odious 18B, carried to a horrible excess. The family is gathered around the fireside to enjoy the scanty fruits of their toil and to recruit their exhausted strength by the little food that they have been able to gather. There they sit. Suddenly there is a knock at the door, and a heavily armed policeman appears. He is not, of course, one who resembles in any way those functionaries whom we honour and obey in the London streets. It may be that the father or son, or a friend sitting in the cottage, is called out and taken off into the dark, and no one knows whether he will ever come back again, or what his fate has been. All they know is that they had better not inquire. There are millions of humble homes in Europe at the moment, in Poland, in Czechoslovakia, in Austria, in Hungary, in Yugoslavia, in Rumania, in Bulgaria—where this fear is the main preoccupation of the family life. President Roosevelt laid down the four freedoms, and these are expressed in the Atlantic Charter which we agreed together. "Freedom from fear"—but this has been interpreted as if it were only freedom from fear of invasion from a foreign country. That is the least of the fears of the common man. His patriotism arms him to withstand invasion or go down fighting; but that is not the fear of the ordinary family in Europe tonight. Their fear is of the policeman's knock. It is not fear for the country, for all men can unite in comradeship for the defence of their native soil. It is for the life and liberty of the individual, for the fundamental rights of man, now menaced and precarious in so many lands, that peoples tremble. (*CS*, 7:7213–16)

On November 7, 1945, while speaking up in celebration of the Anglo-American alliance, he observed "that the world outlook is, in several respects, today less promising than it seemed after the German capitulation of 1918, or after the Treaty of Versailles in 1919.... Then, there were much higher hopes of the world's future than there are now." The one ground for hope lay in "the strength and resolve of the United States to play a leading part in world affairs" (*CS*, 7:7242–44).

Eight days later, at Brussels University, Churchill spoke on "The Foundations of Freedom," warning that the struggle for freedom was not over. "The champions of freedom can never afford to sleep," he said. "Intolerance and persecution are no sooner overcome than they return in new shapes" (*CS*, 7:7250). He sounded the same theme the following day in a joint meeting of the Senate and Chamber of Belgium.

> There are certain simple, practical tests by which the virtue and reality of any political democracy may be measured. Does the Government in any country rest upon a free, constitutional basis, assuring the people the right to vote according to their will? Is there the right of free expression of opinion, free support, free opposition, free advocacy, and free criticism of the government of the day? Are there Courts of Justice free from interference by the Executive or from threats of mob violence, and free from all association with particular political parties? Will these Courts administer open and well established laws associated in the human mind with the broad principles of decency and justice? Will there be fair play for the poor as well as for the rich, and for private persons as well as for Government officials? Will the rights of the individual, subject to his duties to the State, be maintained, asserted, and exalted? In short, do the Government own the people, or do the people own the Government?...Above all, there must be tolerance, the recognition of the charm of variety, and the respect for the rights of minorities. (*CS*, 7:7252–53)

Churchill made no mention in this speech of Eastern Europe, but no one who heard it or read it in those days can have missed his point.

By December 1945, there was evident a change in the American outlook. At a meeting of the foreign ministers of Great Britain, the United States, and the Soviet Union in Moscow, James F. Byrnes, the American secretary of state, pursued the same policy of compromise and accommodation evident in Roosevelt's conduct at Teheran and Yalta and in Truman's conduct at Potsdam. At every turn, however, he was undercut by his own staff. Averell Harriman refused a request that he blame delays in organizing the meeting on Ernest Bevin; Charles Bohlen openly criticized his superior to Bevin's secretary; Isaiah Berlin was approached by another staffer who apologized for Byrnes's inadequacy; and George Kennan murmured to his British counterpart in a similar fashion (*IC*, 139–40). It is hard to believe that this took place without a cue from above.

In the immediate aftermath, Byrnes himself moved toward confrontation, encouraging the Iranians to complain to the United Nations Security Council about the Soviets' failure to live up to their treaty obligations—which required the Soviets to withdraw their occupation troops from Iranian Azerbaijan. His purpose was to make this a "test case" for the defense of the rights of small nations against large-state aggressors. By mid-February 1946, the Americans had become more forceful on the matter than the British. For some time, military men such as Admiral William D. Leahy and some of their political counterparts, such as Secretary of the Navy James Forrestal, Averell Harriman, and Assistant Secretary of War John J. McCloy, had favored a firmer policy. They were joined by George Kennan and others in the State Department, and these were opposed by Joseph Davies, former ambassador to the Soviet Union; Secretary of Commerce Henry Wallace; and Left-leaning diplomats such as the old China hands John Carter Vincent and John Service; as well as by prominent administration figures such as Benjamin Cohen, Leo Pasvolsky, and the as-yet-undiscovered Soviet spy Alger Hiss. There was a debate in the press: on one side, in favor of a firmer policy, stood the *New York Times, Time, Life, Harper's,* and the *Washington Star,* and on the other side were to be found the *New York Herald Tribune,* communist-influenced newspapers such as *PM* and the *Chicago Sun,* and left-liberal journals such as the *Nation* and the *New Republic* (the latter then edited by a no-longer-active Soviet spy who was at that very time concealing the espionage engaged in by his erstwhile comrades at Cambridge University: Kim Philby, Donald McLean, and Anthony Blunt).

Truman later claimed that on January 5, 1946, he rebuked Byrnes for his accommodationist policy, and though Byrnes denies the event and there are grounds for wondering whether any such confrontation took place, Truman's claim may be correct: it is hard to believe that Harriman, Bohlen, and Kennan would have undercut Byrnes in Moscow in December 1945 unless something of the sort was in the air. It is striking, however, that the actual policy did not change markedly until early February—after the discovery of a Soviet atomic spy ring in Canada and after an address in which Stalin asserted that communism and capitalism are incompatible, that no peaceful international order is possible in a world divided between the two systems, that the production of iron and steel in the Soviet

Union, "the basic materials of national defence," must therefore be trebled, and that consumer goods "must wait on rearmament." On February 9, George Kennan, the American chargé d'affaires in Moscow, was asked to comment on the speech: the result was his famous "long telegram," which was dispatched on February 22. "Wherever it is considered timely and promising," Kennan predicted, "efforts will be made to advance [the] official limits of Soviet power." "For the moment," he added,

> ...these efforts are restricted to certain neighboring points conceived of here as being of immediate necessity, such as Northern Iran, Turkey, possibly Bornholm. However, other points may at any time come into question, if and as concealed Soviet political power is extended to new areas. Thus, a "friendly" Persian government might be asked to grant Russia a port on [the] Persian Gulf. Should Spain fall under Communist control, questions of a Soviet base at Gibraltar Strait might be activated. But such claims will appear on [the] official level only when [the] unofficial preparation is complete....
> [The power of the Soviet Union], unlike that of Hitlerite Germany, is neither schematic nor adventuristic. It does not work by fixed plans. It does not take unnecessary risks. Impervious to [the] logic of reason, it is highly sensitive to [the] logic of force. For this reason it can easily withdraw—and usually does—when strong resistance is encountered at any point. Thus, if the adversary has sufficient force and makes clear his readiness to use it, he rarely has to do so. If situations are properly handled there need be no prestige-engaging showdowns.

Kennan thought the Soviet Union in comparison with the Western democracies "still by far the weaker force. Thus their success will really depend on [the] degree of cohesion, firmness and vigor which [the] Western World can muster. And this is [the] factor which it is within our power to influence."[4]

Kennan's "long telegram" is often represented as the crucial intervention that shaped subsequent postwar American policy toward the Soviets. In fact, it served primarily to justify and reinforce a policy already arrived at. By the time that the "long telegram" arrived on February 22, the American reorientation was already ten days old. It

---

4. *WSC* VIII 194–95.

started on February 12—after Churchill's arrival in the United States and after Churchill had visited Washington and discussed the upcoming speech with Truman. It is useful to keep in mind that Truman had issued the invitation to Churchill to come to Westminster College in October 1945—well before the reorientation. What is clear is that Truman and his secretary of state, both of whom read the speech before its delivery, deliberately used the occasion to shape public opinion and to send a message to Stalin. Churchill was to send up a trial balloon, and he was to take the political heat. This suited all concerned: the cautious American politicians and the Englishman who had always delighted in taking the heat.

As I said, the reorientation began on February 12. The first straw in the wind was an American deferral of recognition of the Soviet-sponsored Bulgarian and Romanian regimes. That same day, Secretary of State Byrnes instructed the American representative in Vienna to inform the Austrian government that the Soviet Union—and no one else—was the obstacle to a four-power agreement. That same day, he made formal complaint to the Hoxha government in Albania, threatening to withhold recognition. On February 15, he protested the Soviet failure to implement the Potsdam agreement's provision revising Allied Control Council procedures for Bulgaria, Romania, and Hungary. On March 2, he sent Molotov a note accusing the Soviet Union of holding up the economic recovery of Hungary by overburdening it. Two days later, he registered a similar complaint with the Allied Control Council for Austria. By mid-March, he was demanding American representation on the proposed provisional Danubian commission.

On February 22, Byrnes offered firm American support to the government of Iran in its negotiations with the Russians, insisting that the matter could be taken up in the United Nations. In an important and much discussed speech to the Overseas Press Club on February 28, Byrnes made it clear that the United States would approach matters with "patience and firmness" largely through the agency of the United Nations, and he announced America's intention "to defend the Charter" of the United Nations, indicating that she would resist "aggression," whether it "be accomplished by coercion or pressure or by subterfuges such as political infiltrations," and that she would not be prevented from doing so by "the mere legal veto" exercised in the United Nations Security Council. "If we are to be a great power," he said, "we must act as a great power not only in order to secure our own security but in order to preserve the peace of the world....We will not and we cannot stand aloof if force or the threat of force is used contrary to the purposes and principles of the [United Nations] Charter" (*IC*, 172–75). Byrnes did not mention the Soviet Union; he had no need to do so. Everyone who read or heard the speech understood what he had in mind. In any case, someone—perhaps the secretary of state—leaked the full truth. On March 1, *New York Post* columnist Doris Fleeson wrote from Washington: "A stiffening American attitude towards Russia is in prospect ...the evidence will soon be forthcoming." It was, she reported, "in Mr. Truman's conversation with Winston Churchill here and [in] Churchill's subsequent talks in Florida with Secretary Byrnes and Bernard M. Baruch [that] the new program began to take shape" (*IC*, 179–80). Franklin Delano Roosevelt's "algebra" was beginning to impinge on Joseph Stalin's "practical arithmetic."

Churchill's intention was that the two collide head-on and that the latter ultimately be confined within the terms of the former. At Fulton, he spoke of the dangers posed by war and tyranny, and he argued that, for the moment, it would be imprudent to entrust the atomic bomb to the United Nations; he celebrated the "Magna Carta, the Bill of Rights, the Habeas Corpus, trial by jury, the English common law" that, he contended, "find their most famous expression in the American Declaration of Independence," and he called for the establishment of "a special relationship" between the nations that had produced those "title deeds of freedom." Then he issued a warning. "A shadow has fallen upon the scenes so lately lighted by the Allied victory," he said. "Nobody knows what Soviet Russia and its Communist international organization intends to do in the immediate future, or what are the limits, if any, to their expansive and proselytizing tendencies." In prefacing his most incendiary remarks, he spoke warmly of Stalin and of the Russian people, and he conceded Russia's "need to be secure on her western frontiers" against "all possibility of German aggression." Only then did he add, "It is my duty, however,...to place before you certain facts about the present position in Europe."

> From Stettin in the Baltic to Trieste in the Adriatic, an iron curtain has descended across the Continent. Behind that line lie all the capitals of the ancient states of Central and Eastern Europe. Warsaw, Berlin, Prague, Vienna, Budapest, Belgrade, Bucharest and Sofia, all these famous cities and the populations around them lie in what I must call the Soviet sphere, and all are subject in one form or another, not only to Soviet influence but to a very high and, in some cases, increasing measure of control from Moscow. Athens alone—Greece with its immortal glories—is free to decide its future at an election under British, American and French observation. The Russian-dominated Polish Government has been encouraged to make enormous and wrongful inroads upon Germany, and mass expulsions of millions of Germans on a scale grievous and undreamed-of are now taking place. The Communist parties, which were very small in all these Eastern States of Europe, have been raised to pre-eminence and power far beyond their numbers and are seeking everywhere to obtain totalitarian control. Police governments are prevailing in nearly every case, and so far, except in Czechoslovakia, there is no true democracy. (4–9)

Churchill spoke then of Turkey and of Persia, of Berlin, of the United Nations, of communist pressure in Italy and in France, and of the situation in Manchuria before assuming the role of the prophet and adverting to the role that he had played in the 1930s. It was, all in all, a masterful performance.

On the day of the Fulton speech, while Truman was with Churchill at Westminster College, ostentatiously applauding the most controversial parts of the speech, his secretary of state was busy. To George Kennan in Moscow, he sent a cable, asking him to request from the Soviets copies of all the economic agreements they had made with the East European governments, as was required by the Yalta accords. That same day, he had a critical aide-mémoire delivered to the Bulgarian representative in Washington. At the same time, he sent a protest to Molotov against the economic demands that the Russians were then making on China, and he released to the press a collection of diplomatic documents suggesting that the Russians were looting Manchuria and a statement asserting that General MacArthur's authority as supreme Allied commander in Japan extended to all places where there were Japanese forces, including the districts of Manchuria then under effective Russian control. Finally, he sent a strong protest to the Soviet Union regarding Iran, calling for the immediate withdrawal of the Soviet occupation troops as stipulated by the Anglo-Soviet treaty concerning Iran. The day after the Fulton speech, the State Department announced that the United States was planning to return the body of the deceased Turkish ambassador to Istanbul not by plane or by passenger ship, but on board the USS *Missouri*, the most powerful warship in the world. The message was abundantly clear: the United States would insist on the full implementation of all agreements with the Soviet Union, and it would not stand idly by while the Soviets expanded into Manchuria, Iran, and Turkey.[5]

Neither Truman nor Byrnes openly endorsed Churchill's claims: they kept a certain distance, they both denied that they had read his speech in advance of its delivery, and they patiently waited for the public response, hopeful that Americans would rally to Churchill's banner—which, after the initial uproar had died down, most Americans did, especially when Russian intransigence with regard to Iran and subsequent Soviet behavior in Eastern Europe, especially in Czechoslovakia, and elsewhere confirmed that the analysis which Churchill had presented in his address that fateful day at Westminster College had been all too true.

5. For these events and their significance, see *IC*, 180–82.

*Three*

## Moral Principle and Realistic Judgment

DANIEL J. MAHONEY

Winston Churchill's famous speech on March 5, 1946, delivered at Westminster College in Fulton, Missouri, is popularly known as the "Iron Curtain" speech, though he preferred the more affirmative title of "The Sinews of Peace." The speech is widely recognized as one of Churchill's most important acts of statesmanship and is credited with defining the moral and strategic purposes of the Western alliance during the cold war. Some "revisionist" historians see it as an opening salvo in the cold war. In their view it exacerbated divisions between the wartime Allies and helped transform suspicions into the implacable hostility characteristic of East-West relations during the earliest and coldest period of the cold war. This view, held today only by a dwindling number of intransigent anti-anticommunists, was widely shared at the time by important sectors of the "fellow-traveling" establishment, such as the *Times* of London, and by influential American journals of opinion, such as the *Nation* and the *New Republic*. All of them fiercely denounced Churchill's speech as an unwarranted provocation and a threat to Allied solidarity and international peace. In Britain, ninety-three Labour M.P.'s went so far as to introduce a motion to censure Churchill! In the United States, even President Harry Truman, who accompanied Churchill to Fulton and was generally in sympathy with his message, felt compelled, as a result of the storm unleashed by Churchill's address, to dissemble when he was asked if he had been familiar with its contents prior to its delivery.[1] These distempered contemporary reactions to what in retrospect reads as a lucid presentation of the common sense of the matter cannot help but jar the contemporary reader. But perhaps this contrast should serve to remind us of the extent and depth of the illusions about communism and Soviet intentions that obtained and persisted in many prominent intellectual and even political circles for far too long, as well as to highlight the exceptional good sense that marked Churchill's judgment on the defining issues of war and peace and freedom and tyranny in our century.

Others have traced the salutary role that Churchill's speech played in fortifying the foreign policy of the Truman administration, already alarmed by the Sovietization of Eastern and Central Europe and by Soviet aggressiveness toward Greece and Turkey and threats to the territorial integrity of Persia. It is also widely appreciated today that the Fulton speech played a crucial role in educating both elite opinion and the wider general public in the English-speaking world about the nature of the emerging postwar international "order." Finally, more than any other Anglo-American statesman, Churchill highlighted the possibilities inherent in the "special relationship" between Great Britain and the United States and articulated the moralized realism or, if one prefers, tough-minded idealism that would inspire the creation of the greatest instrument of democratic collective security ever designed, the North Atlantic Treaty Organization (NATO), established in 1949.

Let us turn, however, from these well-known consequences to a discussion of the principles that underlay Churchill's analysis and that made his recommendations so compelling, at least in the long run. Today, with the end of the cold war, it is of course necessary to place these events in which Churchill played such a crucial role in their proper historical perspective. But we also need to step back to examine

---

1. For an account of the immediate reactions to Churchill's speech, see R. Crosby Kemper III, ed., *Winston Churchill: Resolution, Defiance, Magnanimity, Good Will* (Columbia: University of Missouri Press, 1996), 29–30.

the "political philosophy" that is inseparable from and that gave such moral and political depth to his statesmanship. Churchill, I believe, is finally too important to be left to historians or biographers, or even to specialists. He is the common teacher and shared inheritance of all who believe in the ultimate compatibility of political prudence and democratic self-government.

Considered from the point of view of Churchill's larger political reflection, there is little that is new or innovative in the Fulton address. In fact, the speech is a profound illustration of the fundamental consistency of Churchill's moral and political vision. His recurring themes—such as the threats posed to men and nations by modern war and new forms of tyranny, the dangers of appeasement, the prerequisites of civilization and civil society (and the crucial civilizing and pacifying role of the English-speaking democracies), the material and moral requirements of the "special relationship" between Britain and the United States, and the necessity of moving beyond a precarious balance of power toward a covenant backed by the awesome armed might and technical resources of civilized peoples (his "Arms and the Covenant")—are all abundantly manifested in the Fulton address. How do these fundamental pillars of Churchill's political reflection, which are too often dismissed or ignored as merely ornamental or rhetorical, illustrate the fusion of moral principle and realistic political judgment that marks the grandeur of his thought and action?

## Confronting the "Twin Marauders" of War and Tyranny

In his address Churchill sets out to sketch a broad strategic design or "over-all strategic concept" that could provide the necessary "constancy of mind, persistency of purpose, and the grand simplicity of decision" to the English-speaking peoples, under American leadership, in the postwar world (2). This strategic concept is at the service of a broad humanitarian end: it aims to secure the lives and homes and to protect the freedom of ordinary or "humble folk," who are most vulnerable to the "two gaunt marauders" of "war and tyranny" (3) that have plagued the century. Churchill's tone is that of a humane conservative who knows that ordinary democrats need the guidance and direction of an artful statesmanship if they are not to become victims of political manipulation or mistaken judgments about the nature of the threats to peace and freedom. At the root of the danger to liberal and Western civilization is the malignity of totalitarianism, which had displayed itself in equally virulent fascist and communist forms. At Fulton, Churchill spoke as a statesman who knew that the survival of civilization depends upon the preservation of those free political institutions, constitutional practices, and the edifice of the rule of law that historically had provided unprecedented levels of security and humane governance for "the English-speaking peoples." Accordingly, in this speech he would not highlight the very real weaknesses intrinsic to liberal democracy, those "mass effects" inherent in modern life, that he had analyzed with such acuity in *Thoughts and Adventures*. Churchill's more leisurely essays and *The Gathering Storm*, the first volume of his memoirs, *The Second World War*, analyze the "mediocrity" of modern democracy, its leveling of human excellences, its seeming inability to pursue a coherent strategic design, and its propensity toward wishful thinking and the easy or comfortable course of action.[2] Churchill appreciated democracy's ultimate dependence upon the statesmanship that it seems incapable of cultivating. But Churchill's perspective, like that of Alexis de Tocqueville, was also marked by a powerful sense that the various goods of the human and political world, of civilization itself, depend upon the preservation and strengthening of decent and politically free democratic communities. In his view, constitutional democracy is the "best possible regime" available in the modern world, the "worst form of government except for all the rest," as he once famously quipped. Arthur Koestler, the ex-communist author of *Darkness at Noon*, wrote that in the great struggle between the liberal democracies and the fascist and communist tyrannies in the twentieth century, "a half-truth" was at war with a "total lie." Churchill would not have disagreed with this unflattering judgment, but his immediate responsibility was not to

2. See the essays "Mass Effects in Modern Life" and "Fifty Years Hence," in *Thoughts and Adventures*, by Winston S. Churchill (New York: Norton, 1991), 182–204; and Winston S. Churchill, *The Gathering Storm* (Boston: Houghton Mifflin, 1945), esp. 17–18.

quicken the introspective capacities of democratic man but rather to
fortify his will while sharpening his judgment and sense of reality.
This Churchill did with great success at Fulton.

The Fulton address first called for sustained political and military
cooperation as well as "fraternal association" among the "English-
speaking peoples" (6). This great English patriot and intrepid de-
fender of the British Empire was willing to pass leadership of the free
world to the United States partly out of necessity (the baton of leadership had, in fact, already been passed to the United States) but
mainly because he believed that the principles of civilian rule, rule of
law, security for religious and civil liberties, and democratic self-government that would be protected by American leadership and hegemony were more fundamental in the end than British pride or the
preservation of every iota of British sovereignty and imperial power.

This willingness points to the liberal and capacious character of
Churchill's patriotism. He was, as Conor Cruise O'Brien has suggested,
the last great representative of the Whig version of English history,
which made the story of England coextensive with the victory and con-
solidation of the constitution of liberty.[3] In this "Burkean" view, America was simply the completion and perhaps the rationalization and
universalization of a tradition of prescriptive liberties that finds its origin
in the Magna Carta, its development in the great constitutionalist legislation that followed the Glorious Revolution of 1688 (including the
Bill of Rights and Habeas Corpus), and its daily currency and utility in
the tradition of common law. In this view, "the rights of man" or the
"natural and imprescriptible" rights of each human being are a consequence of a tradition of civilized governance that arose in the British
Isles and took distinctive root in the American colonies, but finally have
universal relevance to the dignity of man as man. Of the American Declaration of Independence, Churchill said that it is the "most famous expression" of "the great principles of freedom and the rights of man
which are the joint inheritance of the English-speaking world" (5).
Churchill's understanding of civilization thus synthesizes a Whig view of
the English constitution with an American emphasis on the naturalness

---

3. Conor Cruise O'Brien, *The Great Melody: A Thematic Biography of Edmund
Burke* (Chicago: University of Chicago Press, 1982), xl–xli.

and universality of human rights. Contrary to one line of criticism, best expressed by the Canadian political philosopher George Grant, there is nothing ethnocentric or even narrowly provincial about Churchill's approach to politics or his understanding of liberty or civilization. Rather, Churchill presents a largely Burkean defense of the modern liberal regime in its Anglo-American forms.[4] To paraphrase Lincoln, one might suggest that for Churchill the English-speaking peoples are "mankind's last best hope."

## Preserving Civilization

In the "Iron Curtain" speech Churchill described the institutional and civic features of civilized governance that were threatened by newer, more modern forms of totalitarian and collectivist tyranny:

> ...the people of any country have the right, and should have the power by constitutional action, by free unfettered elections, with secret ballot, to choose or change the character or form of government under which they dwell;...freedom of speech and thought should reign;...courts of justice, independent of the executive, unbiased by any party, should administer laws which have received the broad assent of large majorities or are consecrated by time and custom. Here are the title deeds of freedom which should lie in every cottage home. Here is the message of the British and American peoples to mankind. (5)

Churchill implored the English-speaking peoples to "preach what we practise—let us practise what we preach" (5). He recommended and

---

4. George Grant, *English-Speaking Justice* (South Bend, Ind.: University of Notre Dame Press, 1985). For an illustrative example of Churchill's "Burkean" opposition to "rationalism in politics," see his remarkable "Speech on Rebuilding the House of Commons," October 28, 1943, in Jerry Z. Muller, ed., *Conservatism: An Anthology of Social and Political Thought from David Hume to the Present* (Princeton: Princeton University Press, 1997), 286–89. In this speech, Churchill proposed restoring the House of Commons, destroyed by a German air raid in May 1941, to its original compact "oblong" form rather than building the enlarged "semi-circular" assembly favored by "political theorists." The practical consequence of changing the shape and size of Parliament would be to weaken the party system and to undermine the "conversational style" that had made Parliament "a strong, easy, flexible instrument of free debate." In these matters, Churchill suggested, "logic is a poor guide compared

practiced what Aleksandr Solzhenitsyn has called a "proud, principled and open defense" of human and political liberty.

Such a principled defense of liberty depends, though, upon the cultivation of "civic virtue and manly courage" and "those instruments and agencies of force and science which in the last resort must be the defence of right and reason." These words are drawn from a brief but powerful expression of Churchill's foundational principles presented in a speech called "Civilization," which was delivered at the University of Bristol in the United Kingdom on July 2, 1938.[5]

In that speech Churchill defined civilization as the aspiration toward a peaceful and lawful society, marked by the subordination of warriors and despots to civilian authority. Churchill's Whig "progressivism," if one calls it that, also incorporated an understanding of civilized liberty as a tradition or inheritance that must be safeguarded anew by each generation. He fused a liberal belief in progress with a conservative recognition of the moral and political indispensability of civilizing tradition. He defined the principles of civilization that culminate in a *tradition* of constitutionalism:

> What does it mean? It means a society based upon the opinion of civilians. It means that violence, the rule of warriors and despotic chiefs, the conditions of camps and warfare, of riot and tyranny, give place to parliaments where laws are made, and independent courts of justice in which over long periods those laws are maintained. That is Civilization—and in its soil grow continually freedom, comfort and culture. When Civilization reigns in any country, a wider and less harassed life is afforded to the masses of the people. The traditions of the past are cherished, and the inheritance bequeathed to us by former wise or valiant men becomes a rich estate to be enjoyed and used by all.
>
> The central principle of Civilization is the subordination of the ruling authority to the settled customs of the people and to their will as expressed through the Constitution.[6]

---

with custom." Jerry Muller rightly calls the speech "a minor gem of conservative thought and rhetoric expressing the superiority of historical experience to abstract theory."

5. Winston S. Churchill, "Civilization," in his *Blood, Sweat, and Tears* (New York: G. P. Putnam's Sons, 1941), 45–46.

6. Ibid., 45.

Civilization is not a once-and-for-all achievement, an unearned dispensation of fate, or a product of the march of historical necessity. It is, rather, an inheritance that is always threatened by the atavistic temptations of barbarism and by "the lights of a perverted science," to cite a memorable formulation from Churchill's "Finest Hour" speech on June 18, 1940.

In the peroration of the "Civilization" speech, Churchill also articulated the fundamental principle that he sometimes called "Arms and the Covenant." In this view, the world's peaceful, law-abiding, and liberal nations ought to form larger instruments and organisms of collective security, which would allow international law to be backed by what Thomas L. Pangle has called "a mighty sword in the hand of legal justice." In a world of destructive technology and aggressive ideological despotisms, it is no longer enough to rely on the precarious mechanism of a not always reliable and never automatic balance of power. In words meant to stir the civic virtue and manly courage, as well as the good sense, of Western democrats, Churchill wrote: "Civilization will not last, freedom will not survive, peace will not be kept, unless a very large majority of mankind unite together to defend them and show themselves possessed of a constabulary power before which barbaric and atavistic forces will stand in awe."[7] The idea of "Arms and the Covenant," at the service of the preservation of the inheritance of civilization, is the animating moral and political principle of the Fulton address. The League of Nations, of course, had not lived up to its potential as an instrument of democratic collective security. This failure, exacerbated by the deluded policy of appeasement, helped make what Churchill called "the unnecessary war" more or less inevitable. In the Fulton address, he placed what in retrospect looks to be unmerited confidence in the United Nations Organization (UNO). Even in March 1946, however, he discreetly expressed some foreboding. In his view, the Western democracies, led by the United States and Great Britain, had to provide the firm leadership to guarantee that the UNO was "a reality and not a sham, that it [was] a force for action and not merely a

7. Thomas L. Pangle, *The Ennobling of Democracy: The Challenge of the Postmodern Age* (Baltimore: Johns Hopkins University Press, 1992), 83; Churchill, "Civilization," 46.

frothing of words" (3). Before the democracies cast aside their national armaments, before the pacific and stabilizing American democracy shared the secret of nuclear weaponry with the world organization, it had to be certain that the United Nations was built "upon the rock" and had not degenerated into a pathetic "Tower of Babel" (3).

How perceptive these words seem today to those of us who have witnessed the moral corruption of the United Nations, which for a generation came under the leadership of a coalition of Third World and communist states who paid only lip service to the liberal ideals that had animated the United Nations at its founding! Yet, Churchill refused to give up on the United Nations before it had an opportunity to be tested. He did recommend, in fact, some cautious steps toward the creation of an "international armed force" (4) to be available for use by the United Nations. But it is clear that he did not place excessive hopes in this area. The idea of a "world organization with all the necessary practical safeguards to make it effective" depended upon "the essential brotherhood of man" (4) and on shared liberal political principles and a certain convergence of democratic and constitutionalist political practices. Churchill's idea of a truly effective world organization led by the liberal democracies and dedicated to the international rule of law had something of the same character as Kant's idea of "perpetual peace" guaranteed by a league of free nations: it was, to use the technical language of Kant's philosophy, a regulative "idea of reason" that aimed to encourage substantial progress toward a desirable, if perhaps ultimately unattainable, goal.[8]

Without undermining the widespread, even euphoric confidence placed in the UNO in the early postwar period, Churchill turned his attention to a series of more mundane but perhaps ultimately more realistic and reliable "auxiliary precautions," including the "special relationship" (7) between the United States and the United Kingdom and its Commonwealth of nations; the political, spiritual, and

---

8. Immanuel Kant wrote: "In this manner nature guarantees perpetual peace by the mechanism of human passions. Certainly, she does not do so with sufficient certainty for us to predict the future in any theoretical sense, but adequately from a practical point of view, making it our duty to work toward this end, which is not just a chimerical one" ("Perpetual Peace," in *On History*, trans. Lewis White Beck [New York: Macmillan, 1963], 114).

military recovery of Western Europe; and an anticipation of something like the more localized but effective collective security provided by the Atlantic Alliance. Much of the speech was dedicated, as we have already noted, to an encouragement of the "fraternal association of the English-speaking peoples," an association built upon shared principles and historical experience that promised to culminate in intimate cooperation in the political, scientific, and military fields. Churchill also raised the prospect of what is perhaps another "idea of reason," "the principle of common citizenship" among the English-speaking peoples, though he is content to leave the achievement of this distant goal to "destiny" (7). But Churchill was adamant that this special relationship was in no way incompatible with or corrosive of the ultimate purposes of the United Nations. In fact, he suggested that it was "probably the only means by which that organization [would] achieve its full stature and strength" (7).

In the same spirit, recognizing the multiple concentric embodiments of the principle of "Arms and the Covenant," Churchill cited the words of Christ from the Gospel of John, "In my father's house are many mansions" (7). One of these rooms is a united and pacified democratic Europe dedicated to the principles of the charter of the United Nations. Churchill already anticipated the revival of Europe through the reconciliation and partnership between a "spiritually great France and a spiritually great Germany," which he would announce with great fanfare in his Zurich address on September 19, 1946.[9] In that speech Churchill called for nothing less than the establishment of a "United States of Europe," in which national sovereignties would be pooled in a new federal European system. In his view England would remain outside this new Europe, encouraging it, cooperating with it whenever possible or necessary, but concerned with other global responsibilities and relationships, such as the cultivation of the "special relationship" and the maintenance of the British Commonwealth of Nations. While nothing in Churchill's remarks explicitly called for the creation of an Atlantic Alliance, the structure and purpose of NATO are perfectly compatible with the

9. See "Something that Will Astonish You," Churchill's Zurich speech, in David Cannadine, ed., *Blood, Toil, Tears, and Sweat: The Speeches of Winston Churchill* (Boston: Houghton Mifflin, 1989), 309–14.

Churchillian vision of "Arms and the Covenant" and are a logical response to the Sovietization of East-Central Europe and the increasing weakness of the collective capacities of the United Nations as a result of the obstructionist role played by the totalitarian bloc led by the Soviet Union.

## Communism and the Cold War

The Fulton speech is rightly seen as a call to realistic judgment at a time when public opinion did not wish to admit that the wartime alliance with the Soviet Union had broken down. Its most famous passage lucidly described the communization of half of "liberated" Europe and the consequences for the peace and freedom of Europe:

> From Stettin in the Baltic to Trieste in the Adriatic, an iron curtain has descended across the Continent. Behind that line lie all the capitals of the ancient states of Central and Eastern Europe. Warsaw, Berlin, Prague, Vienna, Budapest, Belgrade, Bucharest and Sofia, all these famous cities and the populations around them lie in what I must call the Soviet sphere, and all are subject in one form or another, not only to Soviet influence but to a very high and, in some cases, increasing measure of control from Moscow. Athens alone—Greece with its immortal glories —is free to decide its future at an election under British, American and French observation. . . . The Communist parties, which were very small in all these Eastern States of Europe, have been raised to pre-eminence and power far beyond their numbers and are seeking everywhere to obtain totalitarian control. (8–9)

Yet, despite the common understanding, this is not the speech of a "cold warrior" in any vulgar sense of the term. Of course, Churchill rejected any and all appeasement of Soviet power and expressed his unyielding opposition to communist totalitarianism, an opposition dating from the establishment of the Soviet regime itself in 1917. Yet, Churchill never called for a policy of liberation or "roll-back" vis-à-vis Soviet power. Instead, he called for the coupling of a policy of military strength on the part of the democracies with an imaginative and vigorous effort to reach "a good understanding on all points with Russia under the general authority of the United Nations Organization" (12). This often overlooked call for a general settlement with the Soviet Union in place of an intensification of the cold war would remain an essential pillar of Churchill's statesmanship in the postwar period, especially during his second tenure as prime minister from 1951 to 1955. It would culminate in his efforts to reach an accommodation with Malenkov and the post-Stalinist leadership in 1953 and 1954, an effort distrusted and never taken seriously by the Eisenhower administration. Perhaps the latter was right in judging that there was a radical contradiction between Churchill's (and by then its own) judgment about the essentially totalitarian and ideological character of the Soviet regime and statecraft and his confidence in the possibility of a general settlement or agreement on East-West issues grounded in common understanding and mutual goodwill. But perhaps the speech offers a clue as to Churchill's ultimate motives and judgment. He told his Fulton audience that the old principle of the balance of power was "unsound" (11). Although Churchill did not agree with an important contemporary school of international relations, which argued that the nature of interstate relations had qualitatively changed in the nuclear age, he certainly believed that history had decidedly slowed down, to use Raymond Aron's apt formulation. My suggestion is that Churchill saw no practical alternative in the nuclear age to the pursuit of détente with the Soviet Union. He reassured himself about the realism of his prescriptions by telling his audience that the Soviet leaders, however totalitarian, were consummate realists and pragmatists as well as convinced ideologues.

Despite his support for a general settlement with Russia, Churchill adamantly rejected two pillars of a more recent "détentist" position. This principled antitotalitarian refused to whitewash or to minimize the ideological or totalitarian nature of the Soviet regime in the name of moral equivalence. He also insisted on the maintenance of military strength on the part of the democracies as the sine qua non for the preservation of both peace and freedom. Rejecting an apolitical and utopian idealism, Churchill never forgot that civilization is an inheritance, which must be defended by armed might and the full force of the scientific tools available to modern man, and that the English-speaking democracies must take the lead in this defense. But he also rejected an equally apolitical and ahistorical realism, which ignored the changes in world politics brought about by mass politics, totalitarian ideologies, and modern technology. Many diplomats and commentators chirped endlessly about the requirements of "the national interest" as if the conditions of international diplomacy remained unchanged from the civilized Machiavellianism that marked the nineteenth-century European cabinets.[10]

## Conclusion

In our new international situation, Churchill provides much-needed theoretical and practical guidance for citizens and statesmen still too often imprisoned by the false dichotomies of realism and idealism. The Fulton address is an ennobling example of Churchill's humane conservatism: a conservatism that appreciated the fragility of civilized institutions and practices and provided an august, perhaps unrepeatable, model of how democratic statesmanship can serve the cause of civilization itself. Even in our posttotalitarian age, there is no evidence that we have arrived at an "end of history." One essential and permanent task of democratic statesmanship undoubtedly remains the protection of the "cottage homes" of humble folk from the twin marauders of war and tyranny. It would be disastrous to assume that never again will they rear their ugly heads.

Without forgetting the necessity and nobility of this task, however, perhaps at this historical moment Churchillians must also confront the systematic erosion of the moral foundations of our democracies that make them worth fighting for in the first place. The statesmanship, speeches, and writings of Churchill provide ample guidance for this complementary task as well.

10. On the unwillingness of many leading realists to confront the inescapably "ideological" character of modern politics, see Raymond Aron, *Peace and War: A Theory of International Relations* (New York: Doubleday, 1966), 90–93, 585–600; and Daniel J. Mahoney, "De Gaulle and the Death of Europe," *National Interest* 48 (summer 1997): 46–49.

A boy from Rolla, Missouri, Scott T. Porter traveled to Fulton with his father, Rev. G. Scott Porter, to see Churchill and Truman, though only his father had a ticket for the speech. "As a 12-year-old," he notes, "I was everywhere.... The motorcade was scheduled to arrive about 1:00 P.M. Its route was easy to determine because of the barriers. I kept moving, looking for what I felt would be a good location from which to photograph the motorcade. In 1946 cameras did not have built-in light meters, automatic focus, or autowind features. You had to do all that before you took your picture. If you were taking an action shot you got one chance and that was it. As only a young boy could do, I found myself in a position in the front row of the crowd when the open car with Churchill and Truman sitting on the back of the seat, surrounded by 'G-men' on the running boards and rear bumper, came driving by. I remember looking at Churchill's left hand when I first got the developed slides back and wondering—was he about to take his cigar out of his mouth or was he about to give the V-for-victory sign? At the time I felt I should have waited a fraction of a second longer to take the picture so I would know—such is the presumption of youth." Porter's photograph shows Winston S. Churchill and Harry S. Truman looking out from their limousine as it turns off Westminster Avenue in Fulton, Missouri, onto Circle Drive on the Westminster College campus about 1:00 P.M., March 5, 1946. Seated directly in front of them is Franc L. "Bullet" McCluer, president of the college; in the front compartment are Admiral William D. Leahy and, to his right, Missouri governor Phil M. Donnelly. Behind the car is West Elementary School, later taken down to make room for the Winston Churchill Memorial and Library. (Photograph by Scott T. Porter, © 1946, 1996, printed by permission of the photographer)

∾ Winston S. Churchill and Harry S. Truman salute the crowd from their special train as Major General Harry H. Vaughan, military aide at the White House, looks on. (Photograph by Abbie Rowe, National Park Service; reproduced courtesy of the Harry S. Truman Library)

84

⌒ Winston S. Churchill and Harry S. Truman on parade through Fulton, Missouri, accompanied by Westminster College president Franc L. "Bullet" McCluer, seated at rear, and, in the front compartment, Admiral William D. Leahy and, to his right, Missouri governor Phil M. Donnelly, March 5, 1946. (Reproduced by permission of the Winston Churchill Memorial and Library, Westminster College, Fulton, Missouri)

↜ Harry S. Truman, Winston S. Churchill, and Westminster College president Franc L. "Bullet" McCluer walking to Washington West House on the college campus, March 5, 1946. In the rear, between Truman and Churchill, is Missouri governor Phil M. Donnelly. The building behind them is Swope Chapel, the old college chapel. (Reproduced by permission of the Winston Churchill Memorial and Library, Westminster College, Fulton, Missouri)

∽ Winston S. Churchill delivers his "Iron Curtain" speech, "The Sinews of Peace," in the gymnasium of Westminster College as Harry S. Truman listens, March 5, 1946. At left is Captain Clark Clifford, the president's naval aide. Behind Truman is Major General Harry H. Vaughan. The man between Truman and Churchill is unidentified. (Reproduced by permission of the Winston Churchill Memorial and Library, Westminster College, Fulton, Missouri)

33.

From Stettin in the Baltic
to Trieste in the Adriatic,

an iron curtain has descended
across the Continent.

Behind that line
lie all the capitals of the ancient states
of Central and Eastern Europe.

Warsaw, Berlin, Prague, Vienna, Budapest,
Belgrade, Bucharest and Sofia,

all these famous cities and the populations
around them

lie in the Soviet sphere

and all are subject
in one form or another,

not only to Soviet influence
but to a very high and increasing
measure of control fr Moscow.

Winston S. Churchill's speaking notes from the page of "The Sinews of Peace" in which he describes the "iron curtain," in Speech notes, Fulton, Mar. 5, 1946, CP 5/4, Churchill Archives Centre, Churchill College, Cambridge. (Reproduced by permission of the estate of Sir Winston S. Churchill)

꙰ "Fulton's Finest Hour, Tuesday, March 5, 1946." Cartoon by Daniel R. Fitzpatrick, *St. Louis Post-Dispatch*, March 5, 1946, 2B. (Reproduced by permission of the *St. Louis Post-Dispatch*)

〜 All eyes on Fulton. Cartoon by Karl Kae Knecht, *Evansville (Ind.) Courier*, March 6, 1946. (Reproduced by permission of the University of Evansville)

⌒ From left to right, the Churchill party on his trip to America: Sarah Churchill, Winston S. Churchill, Clementine S. Churchill, and Randolph S. Churchill at the Statler Hotel, Washington, D.C., March 1946. The man at left is unidentified. (Photograph by Cecil W. Stoughton, later White House photographer during the Kennedy administration; reproduced by permission of the International Churchill Society [United States])

～ Margaret Thatcher delivering the John Findley Green Foundation Lecture, "New Threats for Old," fifty years after Winston Churchill's "Iron Curtain" speech, in Champ Auditorium at Westminster College, Fulton, Missouri, March 9, 1996. (Reproduced by permission of the Winston Churchill Memorial and Library, Westminster College, Fulton, Missouri)

## Four

## A Philosophy of International Politics

SPENCER WARREN

Winston Churchill's "Iron Curtain" speech, delivered in the gymnasium of Westminster College, in Fulton, Missouri, on March 5, 1946, is renowned as one of the greatest and most significant speeches of the twentieth century. It was made at a pregnant moment in history, as America's wartime alliance with Stalin's Soviet Russia was beginning to turn in the direction of cold war. Behind its carefully wrought words lay a half century of Churchill's study and observation of international politics, and a philosophy whose roots can be traced to some of the great thinkers of the seventeenth and eighteenth centuries.

What may be less remembered today is that the address brought down on Churchill a torrent of controversy. Much of this criticism drew its roots from philosophic assumptions quite different from Churchill's. From the comfortable chair of hindsight, more than fifty years later, it should be instructive to compare the views and underlying philosophies of Churchill and his critics as a means of testing them in the light of empirical results. This is not merely an academic exercise, for the main issues discussed by Churchill—the place of the United Nations in what many hoped would be a new world order, control of weapons of mass destruction, and the role of power in ensuring peace—animate foreign policy debate in our post–cold war world much as they did at the dawn of that earlier age.

## The "Iron Curtain" Speech

Following his unexpected and personally devastating defeat in the general election of July 1945, Churchill received many hundreds of invitations to lecture. One came to him in October 1945 from President Truman, who forwarded a letter from Franc L. McCluer, president of Westminster College in Truman's home state. Truman penned on McCluer's letter, "Hope you can do it. I'll introduce you." Churchill wrote to Prime Minister Attlee's private secretary, T. L. Rowan, seeking the government's opinion of his proposed visit. He noted that he and Mrs. Churchill had been invited to stay in Florida for a "couple of months" early in the new year, and that if President Truman accompanied him, "I would certainly feel it my duty . . . to give them an address, of course without any fee." Churchill sent Truman his tentative acceptance in November, and arrived in New York aboard the *Queen Elizabeth* on January 14, 1946, traveling directly to Florida on holiday.[1]

Seven weeks later, Churchill joined Truman in Washington for the trip to Missouri. Disembarking at Jefferson City following the day and night train journey, Churchill and Truman traveled through the state capital briefly by open car; they then drove the twenty-four miles to Fulton in closed cars. On reaching Fulton, whose population of sixty-five hundred had swelled to thirty thousand for the festive day, they sat on the back seat of an open limousine and waved to the crowds filling the streets, rooftops, and windows along the flag-bedecked route. Following a luncheon, Churchill, wearing the scarlet cap and gown of an Oxford doctor, and Truman, in black gown, joined an academic procession into the college gymnasium, where two thousand dignitaries, faculty, students, and other guests were

1. See Henry B. Ryan, "Churchill's 'Iron Curtain' Speech," *Historical Journal* 22:4 (1979): 895–920; *WSC* VIII 190–206; Robert J. Donovan, *Conflict and Crisis: The Presidency of Harry S. Truman, 1945–1948* (New York: Norton, 1977), 190–92.

seated. After Truman's introduction, Churchill began his address, which was broadcast to a national radio audience.[2]

Churchill first set the scene, observing: "The United States stands at this time at the pinnacle of world power. It is a solemn moment for the American Democracy. For with primacy in power is also joined an awe-inspiring accountability to the future" (2). He spoke of the paramount goal of protecting the people in their "myriad cottage or apartment homes" from "the two gaunt marauders, war and tyranny" (2–3). He then turned to the need to prevent, first, war— by means of the new United Nations:

> We must make sure that its work is fruitful, that it is a reality and not a sham, that it is a force for action and not merely a frothing of words, that it is a true temple of peace in which the shields of many nations can some day be hung up, and not merely a cockpit in a Tower of Babel. Before we cast away the solid assurances of national armaments for self-preservation we must be certain that our temple is built, not upon shifting sands or quagmires, but upon the rock. (3)

Churchill's "rock" was organized armed force. Just as courts cannot function without sheriffs, the United Nations "must immediately begin to be equipped with an international armed force" (4). As a first step, he suggested that each state delegate a certain number of air squadrons to the United Nations; they would remain national forces but be directed by the world body.

But when Churchill turned to another major issue of the day, he unhesitatingly endorsed the West's monopoly of the atomic bomb, emphasizing his opposition to entrusting U.S. and British knowledge of its secrets to the United Nations "while it is still in its infancy. It would be criminal madness to cast it adrift in this still agitated and un-united world," he warned (4). No country had slept less well because the knowledge and method of building the bomb were held in American hands, but they would not have slept so soundly had "some Communist or neo-Fascist State monopolized for the time being these dread agencies" (4). The parallel of communist and fascist must have been jarring to some listeners at a time when Soviet Russia was still seen as our wartime partner. Churchill

2. *Newsweek*, Mar. 18, 1946, 30–31.

continued: "God has willed that this shall not be and we have at least a breathing space to set our house in order before this peril has to be encountered: and even then, if no effort is spared, we should still possess so formidable a superiority as to impose effective deterrents upon its employment, or threat of employment, by others." The atomic secret could be confided to the United Nations, said Churchill, only "when the essential brotherhood of man is truly embodied" in that institution, "with all the necessary practical safeguards to make it effective" (4). President Truman was among those applauding at this point.[3]

Prevention of tyranny, the second of the two marauders, was Churchill's next subject. He alluded to Russian-sponsored repression in Eastern Europe, where "the power of the State is exercised without restraint, either by dictators or by compact oligarchies operating through a privileged party and a political police. It is not our duty at this time when difficulties are so numerous to interfere forcibly in the internal affairs of countries which we have not conquered in war," Churchill stated, but "we must never cease to proclaim in fearless tones the great principles of freedom and the rights of man which are the joint inheritance of the English-speaking world. . . ." Here he made the first reference to his enduring theme of Anglo-American kinship (which he had laid out in an address at Harvard in 1943), noting that the Magna Carta and the other great symbols of English liberty "find their most famous expression in the American Declaration of Independence." These "title deeds of freedom" should be "the message of the British and American peoples to mankind" (5).

Political liberty also rests on economic progress. Churchill observed that poverty and privation were to many the "prevailing anxiety" in that bleak first postwar year. He foresaw that "science and co-operation" (the latter possibly an allusion to the Bretton Woods agreements of 1944–1945) would bring in the next few decades "an expansion of material well-being beyond anything that has yet occurred in human experience." The "hunger and distress which are the aftermath of our stupendous struggle" will pass, he averred, "and

3. *Times* (London), Mar. 7, 1946, 4.

there is no reason except human folly or sub-human crime which should deny to all the nations the inauguration and enjoyment of an age of plenty" (5–6).

Now Churchill reached his first main message, what he called the "crux," of his address: "Neither the sure prevention of war, nor the continuous rise of world organization will be gained without what I have called the fraternal association of the English-speaking peoples. This means a special relationship between the British Commonwealth and Empire and the United States of America" (6). He then outlined his concept of this relationship in terms of continued wartime military cooperation and joint use of bases. The principle of the Permanent Defense Agreement between the United States and Canada should be extended to all in the Commonwealth, leading eventually, he hoped, to common citizenship. Until then, Churchill was concerned to build a special Anglo-American relationship, both to ensure continued U.S. involvement in the world (assisting Britain to counter Soviet power) and to help maintain the position of a depleted and exhausted postwar Britain.[4]

Churchill pursued his theme at Fulton with delicacy, taking care not to use the word *alliance* (though his meaning was evident, and

4. In hindsight, one could argue that in looking across the Atlantic Ocean to maintain Britain as a great power, as he had done with such success in the war, Churchill overlooked a more realistic role for Britain as the leader of a revived Europe, when such a role was hers for the asking. Churchill in the early postwar years was an eloquent proponent of European unity, based on a reconciliation between France and Germany, but he wanted Britain to stand apart. When she finally joined Europe twenty-five years later, under much reduced circumstances, she had missed the opportunity to help shape the new community at its birth. To be fair, however, detailed involvement in Europe was against the whole tradition of British foreign policy, and Churchill's romantic vision of a continuing worldwide role for Britain was essentially shared by the Attlee government and most other British officials at the time. (They knew, for example, that British trade with the Commonwealth exceeded that with Europe.) Nor would most British politicians in the 1940s countenance the federalist notions propounded then by French Europeanists any more than many will today. See Robin Edmonds, *Setting the Mould: The United States and Britain, 1945–1950* (New York: Norton, 1986), 209, 253–54; John W. Young, "British Officials and European Integration," in *Building Postwar Europe*, ed. Anne Deighton (New York: St. Martin's Press, 1995). See also Stuart Croft, "British Policy towards Western Europe, 1947–1949: The Best of Possible Worlds?" *International Affairs* 64:4 (autumn 1988): 617–29; and Jan Melissen and Bert Zeeman, "Britain and Western Europe, 1945–1951: Opportunities Lost?" *International Affairs* 63:1 (winter 1986/1987): 81–95.

many headlines used the term). He knew his American history and the country's idealistic, decidedly un-British (and in some respects anti-British) tradition in foreign affairs. He had been a senior member of the British government twenty-seven years before, when America and the world also stood at a "solemn moment" in history. He had recounted in *The World Crisis*, his history of the First World War, how President Wilson's dream of a new world order, abolishing alliances and the old power politics in favor of a world organization, had crashed in disaster. He knew the United States had never joined a peacetime alliance and had little appetite for entanglement outside the Western hemisphere. He knew all too well the immense difficulty with which President Roosevelt had endeavored to break down his people's isolationist impulse, on which effort Britain's very life had depended in 1940–1941.

Thus, deeply mindful of the sensibilities of his audience, Churchill subtly joined his concept of the "special relationship" to the American romance with the United Nations. Rejecting the view that such a relationship between the two countries would contradict the principle of world unity through the United Nations, he insisted that, "on the contrary, it is probably the only means by which that organization will achieve its full stature and strength." He then noted U.S. ties to the South American republics and Britain's twenty-year treaty with Russia; special, nonaggressive associations were "indispensable" (7).

Why should not the "Temple of Peace," Churchill asked, which is being built by workmen from all countries, be assisted by workmen from two who happen to "know each other particularly well and are old friends"? "Why can they not share their tools and thus increase each other's working powers?" (7).

From this metaphor of hope, slightly more than halfway through his speech, Churchill invoked a specter of darkness. For if the two workmen who know each other so well do not work together, then

> the temple may not be built, or, being built, it may collapse, and we shall all be proved again unteachable and have to go and try to learn again for a third time in a school of war, incomparably more rigorous than that from which we have just been released. The dark ages may return, the Stone Age may return on the gleaming wings of science, and what might now shower immeasurable

material blessings upon mankind may even bring about its total destruction. Beware, I say; time may be short. (8)

Churchill now reached the second message of his address, sounding an urgent alarm at the threat posed by the two countries' wartime ally, Soviet Russia: "A shadow has fallen upon the scenes so lately lighted by the Allied victory. Nobody knows what Soviet Russia and its Communist international organization intends to do in the immediate future, or what are the limits, if any, to their expansive and proselytizing tendencies." Churchill then paused to express his "strong admiration and regard for the valiant Russian people" and for his "wartime comrade, Marshal Stalin." He accepted "the Russian need to be secure on her western frontiers" against Germany. He welcomed Russia to "her rightful place among the leading nations of the world" and especially "constant, frequent and growing contacts" (8) with the Russian people—the latter hardly something that would appeal to Stalin.

Having made that bow, Churchill cast aside all indirection and allusion to set forth "certain facts about the present position in Europe": "From Stettin in the Baltic to Trieste in the Adriatic, an iron curtain has descended across the Continent" (8).[5] The Russians had imposed varying measures of central control from Moscow, and their communist parties "are seeking everywhere to obtain totalitarian control." He then noted Moscow's pressure against both Turkey and Persia.

---

5. An early use of this vivid image was made in 1918 by the Russian emigré philosopher Vasiliy Rozanov, who wrote in his book, *Apocalypse of Our Time:* "With a rumble and a roar, an iron curtain is descending on Russian history." Lady Snowden, wife of the Labour Party figure Philip Snowden, described her arrival with a Labour delegation in the new Soviet Union in 1920: "We were behind the 'iron curtain' at last!" In February 1945, Joseph Goebbels wrote in *Das Reich* that if Germany surrendered, "an iron curtain would at once descend" on Eastern Europe and part of the Reich. Nine days before Churchill first used the term in a May 12, 1945, telegram to Truman, the German foreign minister, Count Schwerin von Krosigk, was reported in the *Times* (London) as having told the German people in a broadcast: "In the East the iron curtain behind which, unseen by the eyes of the world, the work of destruction goes on, is moving steadily forward." Churchill next employed the words in another telegram to Truman on June 4. He first used it publicly in Parliament on August 16, 1945. On November 15, 1945, Senator Arthur Vandenberg warned against the "iron curtain of secrecy" the Soviets had drawn. Sources can be found in *WSC* VIII 7 and Ryan, "Churchill's 'Iron Curtain' Speech," 897–98.

(The Russians were demanding cession of two Turkish provinces, Kars and Ardahan, as well as a base in the Bosporus, and in violation of a wartime agreement were refusing to withdraw their troops from Iran; they had also set up an autonomous regime in Iranian Azerbaijan.) Churchill also charged the Russians with building a procommunist regime in their German occupation zone; instead what was needed was a "new unity in Europe"—including prostrate Germany— "within," he was sure to add, "the structure of the United Nations" (9–10). He then listed other threats: communist strength in Italy and France, communist fifth columns in many countries far from Russia taking direction from Moscow, and the continuing Red Army occupation of Manchuria.

But war was not inevitable, or even imminent. "I do not believe that Soviet Russia desires war," said Churchill. "What they desire is the fruits of war and the indefinite expansion of their power and doctrines" (11). A "settlement" was needed, Churchill asserted, as he turned to his third message, his philosophy of power. Of the Russians, he maintained, "there is nothing they admire so much as strength, and there is nothing for which they have less respect than for weakness, especially military weakness. For that...reason the old doctrine of a balance of power is unsound" (11).

In thus dismissing the key concept of traditional diplomacy, was Churchill agreeing with the Wilsonian rejection of Old World power politics? Hardly. He had a different concept of power, neither fully traditional nor Wilsonian: "We cannot afford...to work on narrow margins, offering temptations to a trial of strength. If the Western Democracies stand together in strict adherence to the principles of the United Nations Charter, their influence for furthering those principles will be immense and no one is likely to molest them" (11–12). Before making a more direct statement of his concept of power, Churchill thus once again covered his strong pill of Anglo-American power with the sugarcoating of the United Nations, under whose "general authority" an understanding with Russia could be achieved (12).

Finally, Churchill reached his peroration: "If the population of the English-speaking Commonwealths be added to that of the United States, with all that such co-operation implies in the air, on the sea, all over the globe, and in science and in industry, and in moral force, there will be no quivering, precarious balance of power to offer its temptation to ambition or adventure. On the contrary, there will be an overwhelming assurance of security" (12–13). In short, Churchill's concept of power—"an overwhelming assurance of security"— meant Anglo-American superiority over Soviet Russia. (He listed air and sea power here ahead of science and morals.) This principle rested on a simple observation: the *balance* of power had twice broken down in Europe within a quarter of a century; *superiority*, then, was the best safeguard against a third breakdown, which would end in atomic catastrophe.

Churchill found it impolitic to say "superiority" in his closing, but he did employ it earlier in the speech with reference to atomic weapons. And in May 1944 he had said the new world body should be armed to ensure that "within the limits assigned to it, it has overwhelming military power."[6] He concluded thus:

> If we adhere faithfully to the Charter of the United Nations and walk forward in sedate and sober strength, seeking no one's land or treasure, seeking to lay no arbitrary control upon the thoughts of men; if all British moral and material forces and convictions are joined with your own in fraternal association, the highroads of the future will be clear, not only for us but for all, not only for our time, but for a century to come. (13)

The combined strength of the English-speaking peoples constituted "The Sinews of Peace," Churchill's title for his address.

## Background and Response to the Fulton Address

Churchill spoke in a climate of increasingly anxious U.S.-Soviet relations. U.S. policy was already taking early steps away from the late

6. *Parliamentary Debates*, Commons, 5th ser., vol. 400 (1944), cols. 785–86. In a May 1937 speech to the New Commonwealth Society, Churchill said, "We are one of the few peace societies that advocates the use of force, if possible overwhelming force, to support public international law" (Winston S. Churchill, *Complete Speeches, 1897–1963*, ed. Robert Rhodes James, 8 vols. [New York: Chelsea House, 1974], 6:5855 [hereinafter cited as *Speeches*]). And in March 1936, Churchill said, "I desire to see the collective forces of the world invested with overwhelming power" (*Parliamentary Debates*, Commons, 5th ser., vol. 310 (1936), col. 1530.

President Roosevelt's accommodationist policy toward Soviet Russia, which his successor had generally continued, in the direction of a more confrontational policy. Stalin's "Election" speech on February 9, 1946, had created concern in Washington and London with its emphasis on the opposition between socialism and capitalism, whose internal contradictions, Stalin said, had precipitated the war and threatened to set off another.[7] On February 15, news of a Russian atomic spy ring in Canada was officially confirmed with the detention of twenty-two people.[8] (It had been known to the U.S. government since September.)[9] Although it was not public, George Kennan's subsequently famous "long telegram" had been sent from the U.S. embassy in Moscow to the State Department on February 22 and was receiving wide circulation in the government. President Truman was among its readers. (Kennan later described the reaction as "nothing less than sensational.")[10]

These and other events were making a sharp impact on public opinion. The first meeting of the United Nations General Assembly had recently ended in London. Secretary of State James F. Byrnes, who headed the U.S. delegation, had been under pressure for being too soft on the Russians. He signaled a more robust U.S. attitude in a February 28 speech to the Overseas Press Club at the Waldorf=Astoria, criticizing continued Russian occupation of northern Iran, its role in setting up an autonomous regime in Iranian Azerbaijan, and confiscation of industrial equipment in Eastern Europe and Manchuria. Byrnes warned, "We cannot overlook a unilateral gnawing away at the status quo [or] allow aggression to be accomplished by coercion or pressure or by subterfuges such as political infiltration." (A week later, on the day of Churchill's speech, the State Department made public its dispatch of two notes to Moscow protesting Russian actions in Iran and Manchuria.)[11]

7. For the text, see Robert V. Daniels, *A Documentary History of Communism*, 2 vols. (New York: Vintage Books, 1960), 2:142–47.

8. *New York Times*, Feb. 16, 1946, 1.

9. Hugh Thomas, *Armed Truce* (New York: Atheneum, 1987), 195–96.

10. George F. Kennan, *Memoirs, 1925–1950* (Boston: Little, Brown, 1967), 294. The text of the "long telegram" can be found in *Foreign Relations of the United States* (1946), 6:696–709.

11. *New York Times*, Mar. 6, 1946, 1.

But Byrnes did not wish to sound too harsh. He did not criticize Soviet Russia by name and continued to stress the importance of maintaining the "unity of all great powers" and preventing "exclusive blocs or spheres of influence." "We must live by the Charter," he insisted. "That is the only road to peace."[12]

The day before Byrnes spoke, Senator Arthur Vandenberg, a Byrnes critic, asked in a Senate speech, "What is Russia up to now?" He too urged a stronger U.S. stand but, like Byrnes, stressed working for peace through the United Nations.[13] The "Week in Review" section of the Sunday *New York Times* of March 3, 1946, headlined its analysis, "Is Our Policy Changing?" and James B. Reston's article was titled, "Have We a New Foreign Policy? Capital Asks."

In retrospect, it appears Truman was allowing Churchill to encapsulate events and crystallize opinion on behalf of a new policy that was already taking effect.[14] Churchill had discussed his speech with Truman at a White House meeting on the evening of February 10 (and earlier on February 7 in Havana with the U.S. minister there, who forwarded his account directly to Truman), and also with Byrnes and Bernard Baruch in Florida on February 17. Truman also saw the speech on the train journey to Missouri, and Byrnes read it in full before their departure.[15] *Time* perceptively wrote that for Truman, Churchill's speech was a "magnificent trial balloon."[16]

But Churchill's harsh, even gloomy, tone and the breadth and detail with which he made his case—the first strong criticisms of Russia by a Western leader since the Nazi invasion of Russia in June 1941—brought down on him a torrent of controversy. (Actually, it brought him back to the stage he had known all of his career except for the war years.) Senators Claude Pepper, Hardy Kilgore, and Glenn Taylor issued a joint statement: "Mr. Churchill's proposal would cut the

12. Ibid., Mar. 1, 1946, 10.

13. *Congressional Record*, 79th Cong., 2d sess., 1946, 92, pt. 2:1692–95.

14. Beginning in mid-February, the State Department took a number of steps to stiffen U.S. policy in Eastern Europe, Iran, and Turkey. See Fraser J. Harbutt, *The Iron Curtain: Churchill, America, and the Origins of the Cold War* (New York: Oxford University Press, 1986), 165–70.

15. See ibid., 161–62; Ryan, "Churchill's 'Iron Curtain' Speech," 903–10; and *WSC* VIII 192, 197.

16. *Time*, Mar. 18, 1946, 19.

throat of the United Nations Organization" (as it was then known).[17] Representative Jerry Patterson railed against the speech, claiming that Churchill was asking "that we should revert to the reactionary and self-destructive...old idea of balancing of one power or one group of powers against another group....Blocs of powers against powers in this atomic age can only bring world war and total destruction to the human race."[18]

Nobel Prize laureate Pearl Buck called Churchill's visit a "catastrophe." George Bernard Shaw believed that Churchill's speech was "nothing short of a declaration of war on Russia" and that Churchill was proposing a "recrudescence of the old balance of power policy... with a view to a future war."[19] The *Chicago Sun* denounced his "poisonous doctrines."[20] Marquis Childs wrote in the *Washington Post* that the speech "overlooks a vital truth...that...you cannot fight the 'Communist menace' by armed alliances." Rather, Childs maintained, the world needed to address the root economic and social causes of popular discontent.[21] In the House of Commons, 105 M.P.'s introduced a motion condemning the speech and affirming the view "that world peace and security can be maintained not by sectional alliances, but by progressively strengthening the power and authority of U.N.O. to the point where it becomes capable of exercising...the functions of a world government."[22]

Leading liberal newspapers and magazines attacked Churchill for relying on the old power politics, endangering the United Nations, and wrongly placing the blame on Russia. Norman Cousins wrote in the *Saturday Review* that "Russian unilateralism today is not *the* disease; it is a product of the disease." The danger "is the centuries-old problem of competitive national sovereignties..., the race for security, each nation deciding for itself what is necessary for its own security...." This leads to military bases, spheres of influence, alliances, and the arms race, all of which in the past had led to war. The only hope, he concluded, mindful of the atomic bomb, "is *real* world organization,

17. *New York Times*, Mar. 7, 1946, 1.
18. *Congressional Record*, 79th Cong., 2d sess., 1946, 92, pt. 2:1970.
19. *New York Times*, Mar. 7, 1946, 5.
20. *Chicago Sun*, Mar. 6, 1946, quoted in *U.S. News*, Mar. 15, 1946, 39.
21. *Washington Post*, Mar. 6, 1946, 10.
22. *Parliamentary Debates*, Commons, 5th ser., vol. 420 (1946), col. 1293.

meaning world law...."[23] The *New Republic* proclaimed, "Security is found in the hatred of all peoples for war, and the demand of all peoples that all issues between nations be resolved through the U.N.O.... One standard must be raised now... '*Stand by the Charter.*' "[24]

For their part, conservative critics were more concerned with Churchill's proposal of a peacetime Anglo-American alliance than with his attacks on Russian policy. Senator Robert Taft agreed with much of Churchill's criticism of Russia, but he believed "It would be very unfortunate for the U.S. to enter into any military alliance with England, Russia, or any other country in time of peace." Senator George Aiken commented: "I'm not ready to enter a military alliance with anyone. Britain, the United States and Russia should pull together to make the United Nations work."[25]

Others were concerned about placing the United States in the position of backing British imperialism. The *New York Herald Tribune* wrote that the speech had "miscarried" and noted that "American comment suggests a reluctance to assume responsibility for all British imperial interests."[26] The country's most prestigious columnist, Walter Lippmann, wrote: "The line of the British imperial interest and the line of American vital interest are not to be regarded as identical." He also criticized what he saw as Churchill's call for an anti-Soviet alliance.[27] (In private, he deplored the speech as "a direct incitement to a preventive war" and an "almost catastrophic blunder.")[28] The British embassy in Washington found in its mail that the main criticism was not Churchill's warning against Soviet Russia but what was seen as his call for an anti-Soviet alliance in support of British imperialism.[29]

Although support came from the *New York Times* (rather generally), the *Christian Science Monitor*, *Time*, and the *Philadelphia Inquirer* (but not from many journals beyond the East Coast),[30] and

---

23. *Saturday Review*, Mar. 30, 1946, 28; italics in original.
24. *New Republic*, Mar. 25, 1946, 396; italics in original.
25. *Los Angeles Times*, Mar. 6, 1946, 9.
26. *New York Herald Tribune*, Mar. 7, 1946, 26.
27. Ibid., 25.
28. Ronald Steel, *Walter Lippmann and the American Century* (Boston: Little, Brown, 1980), 429.
29. Ryan, "Churchill's 'Iron Curtain' Speech," 915.
30. *U.S. News*, Mar. 15, 1946, 39.

from columnists such as Ernest K. Lindley of *Newsweek*[31] and George
Fielding Eliot of the *Herald Tribune*,[32] the speech had ignited so much
controversy that *Newsweek* described it as the "worst diplomatic storm
of the postwar period."[33] At a press conference three days after the
speech, President Truman refused to endorse it and wrongly denied
that he knew its contents in advance.[34] Prime Minister Attlee refused to
comment on the speech in response to a question in the House of
Commons.[35] When Churchill visited New York on March 15 for a
Broadway ticker-tape parade on Churchill Day, he was greeted by hundreds of protesters, and Undersecretary of State Dean Acheson
abruptly bowed out of his place as the U.S. representative at Churchill's
address at the Waldorf=Astoria, which, in the event, was unrepentant.[36]

## Churchill's Philosophy of International Politics

Churchill's speech at Fulton was not something pulled together
from headlines and opinion pages, but the product of mature reflection and an impressive consistency of outlook dating back to his
youth. In 1897, at the age of twenty-two, in a letter to his mother
written while serving with the army in India, he explained his efforts
to "build up a scaffolding of logical and consistent views," which was
to be constructed of facts and "muscles," or principles.[37] In 1936 he
stated: "Those who are possessed of a definite body of doctrine and
of deeply rooted convictions...will be in a much better position to
deal with the shifts and surprises of daily affairs than those who are
merely taking short views, and indulging their natural impulses as
they are evoked by what they read from day to day."[38] Near the end
of his political career, in 1953, he commented: "True wisdom is to

31. *Newsweek*, Mar. 18, 1946, 36.
32. *New York Herald Tribune*, Mar. 8, 1946, 21.
33. *Newsweek*, Mar. 25, 1946, 27.
34. *Public Papers and Addresses of Harry S. Truman*, Mar. 8, 1946, 145, hereinafter cited as *Truman Papers*.
35. *Parliamentary Debates*, Commons, 5th ser., vol. 420 (1946), col. 761.
36. *New York Times*, Mar. 15, 1946, 1.
37. *WSC* I 334.
38. Quoted in Winston S. Churchill, *The Gathering Storm* (Boston: Houghton
Mifflin, 1948), 210.

cultivate a sense of proportion which may help one to pick out the three or four things that govern all the rest and as it were write one's own headlines and not change them very often."[39] Among the three or four things governing Churchill's outlook were his view of history as the great teacher and guide; unchanging human nature, which uneasily joins a lust for power with an impulse for liberty; superior power in the hands of civilized states as the guarantor of peace and freedom; and the evolutionary, natural process of politics.

Churchill was keenly aware of man's limitations and skeptical of utopian, rationalistic solutions to age-old problems. Like Edmund Burke and others in the empirical conservative tradition, he saw politics as an organic process in which concrete facts and human nature —as embodied in custom, tradition, and experience—counted for far more than man-made theories, ideological constructions, and legalistic formulas.

## ON THE COLLAPSE OF COMMUNISM

Churchill's philosophy is illustrated by his predictions of the collapse of communism. In January 1920, he predicted it would fail in Russia because it was "fundamentally opposed to the needs and dictates of the human heart, and of human nature itself." He denounced Bolshevism as a "rule of men who in their insane vanity and conceit believe they are entitled to give a government to a people which the people loathe and detest.... The attempt to carry into practice those wild theories can only be attended with universal confusion, corruption, disorder, and civil war." Out of the "bloodshed and foment" of the civil war then raging, Churchill predicted, would emerge not the visionary communist republic, "but something quite different. The ferocious military leaders and artful political wirepullers are the people who emerge in their own interest and the interest of their belongings."[40] In 1931 he wrote that Bolshevism would never work because it was at war with "intractable" human nature and would be unable to control "the explosive variations of its phenomena." In the

39. *Speeches*, 8:8507.
40. *Speeches*, 2:2920–21.

midst of the Great Depression, when many in the West looked long-ingly at the promise of rationalist central planning, Churchill wrote that communism not only had "lost the distinction of individuals," but also had "not even made the nationalization of life and industry pay. We have not much to learn from them, except what to avoid."[41]

Later, in January 1952, at the height of the cold war, Churchill told a joint session of Congress, "I am by no means sure that China will re-main for generations in the Communist grip. The Chinese said of themselves several thousand years ago: 'China is a sea that salts all the waters that flow into it.'"[42] Of the subjugated states of Eastern Europe, he predicted in February 1954: "Time may find remedies that this gen-eration cannot command. The forces of the human spirit and of na-tional character alive in those countries cannot be speedily extinguished, even by large-scale movements of populations and mass education of children." He then contrasted the temporary nature of Stalin's con-quests with other results of his aggression "which will live and last":

> Nothing but the dread of Stalinised Russia could have brought the conception of united Europe from dreamland into the fore-front of modern thought.
>     Nothing but the policy of the Soviets and of Stalin could have laid the foundations of that deep and lasting association which now exists between Germany and the Western world, be-tween Germany and the United States, between Germany and Britain and, I trust, between Germany and France. These are events which will live and which will grow while the conquests and expansion achieved by military force and political machin-ery will surely dissolve or take new and other forms.[43]

41. Winston S. Churchill, "Mass Effects in Modern Life," *Strand* (May 1931): 478, reprinted in Winston S. Churchill, *Thoughts and Adventures* (New York: Nor-ton, 1990), 185–86. Compare the *Times* (London) of Mar. 6, 1946, 5, in a leader that may have been written by E. H. Carr, commenting on the Fulton speech. While communism and the West "are in many respects opposed," it wrote, "they have much to learn from each other—Communism in the ... establishment of individual rights, western democracy in the development of economic and social planning. The ideological warfare between [them] cannot result in an out-and-out victory for ei-ther side."

42. *Speeches*, 8:8326.

43. *Parliamentary Debates*, Commons, 5th ser., vol. 524 (1954), cols. 582–83. On New Year's Day 1953, Churchill predicted to his private secretary, John Colville, that if Colville lived his normal life span, he would see Eastern Europe free of com-munism. Colville was born in 1915 and died in 1987 (Colville, *The Fringes of Power: 10 Downing Street Diaries, 1939–1955* [New York: Norton, 1985], 658).

Finally, in his 1957 epilogue to the one-volume edition of his World War II memoirs, Churchill wrote that Russia's

> people experience every day...those complications and palliatives of human life that will render the schemes of Karl Marx more out of date and smaller in relation to world problems than they have ever been before. The natural forces are working with greater freedom and greater opportunity to fertilise and vary the thoughts and the power of individual men and women. They are far bigger and more pliant in the vast structure of a mighty empire than could ever have been conceived by Marx in his hovel....[H]uman society will grow in many forms not comprehended by a party machine.[44]

How interesting that Churchill's political philosophy enabled him to foretell the collapse of communism when it was at the zenith of its power—as well as at its inception—when most scholars, with all their detailed study, were unable to see this as late as the mid-1980s.[45]

## ON INTERNATIONAL ORGANIZATION

Churchill viewed the United Nations, as he had its predecessor the League of Nations, with skepticism, seeing each as a supplement to national power, as a means of organizing and legitimating the collective power of states, not as an alternative to it. He differed sharply from those who saw first the League and then the United Nations ushering in a new age of cooperation and harmony that would eliminate the requirements of national power.

From the start, Churchill emphasized that the League did not alter the traditional practices of power politics. Two weeks after the end of the First World War, in November 1918, he told his Dundee constituents in an election address that he was all for the League but that it was "no substitute for the supremacy of the British Fleet."[46] As secretary of state for war in March 1919, when the League was

---

44. Winston S. Churchill, *The Second World War*, 1-vol. abridgment (Boston: Houghton Mifflin, 1959), 1015–16.

45. See the articles in part 2, "Sins of the Scholars," in "The Strange Death of Soviet Communism," *National Interest* special issue (spring 1993).

46. *Speeches*, 3:2642.

about to be born at the Versailles peace conference, Churchill deprecated it before the House of Commons: "When we have seen the
real difficulties overcome, then will be the time... —and not till then
—to deprive ourselves of those real securities which, thank God, we
have always wielded in the past, and which we will not, without sufficient substitute, deprive ourselves of in the future."[47]

As chancellor of the exchequer, in December 1924, he told the
Committee of Imperial Defence that he "had never considered that
the League of Nations...was in a position to preserve peace," something that "could only be obtained by the maintenance of good understandings between various groups of Powers, possibly arrived at
under the auspices of the League of Nations." He did not consider
"that people would undertake obligations of an unlimited character
which it was impossible to define." Outlining a theme he was to take
up during the Second World War, Churchill advocated regional
agreements under the League to demilitarize particular points of
danger. His view was based on the recognition that states could be
expected to take action to keep the peace only if their interests were
directly affected, not merely in support of a general principle of collective security. By means of such limited, practical steps, he said,
"the authority of the League would be vastly strengthened."[48]

During the 1930s Churchill naturally turned to the League, and
those of its supporters who favored rearmament, as allies in his resistance to Hitler. He began to speak more strongly in favor of the
world body, but stressed that it must have force behind it and not be
a mere abstraction: "If the idea of force—force in the extreme—is
excluded from the procedure of a League of Nations, it is nought
but an idle sham," he said in July 1936.[49] Collective security, he asserted later that year, was "no substitute for national self defence
[but] might be a great reinforcement of it."[50] Contrarily, many
League supporters, including most of the Labour Party, saw the

47. *Parliamentary Debates*, Commons, 5th ser., vol. 113 (1919), col. 182.
48. *WSC* V C (1) 286–87.
49. *Speeches*, 6:5779. This dilemma has been faced by the United Nations most
clearly in the Balkan and Iraq crises. For all the talk of a "new world order," the
United Nations has had to rely on the ultimate sanction of U.S. power, thus demonstrating Churchill's insight into the limitations of international organization.
50. *Speeches*, 6:5797.

League's multilateralism as a substitute for force and national strength, and opposed rearmament.

Essentially, Churchill saw the League as a twentieth-century Concert of Europe. He viewed the crises of the 1930s through the prism of British interests and the power balance, advocating collective security insofar as it advanced British security, not as an abstract principle. Thus, Churchill did not believe the League had an obligation to act against Japanese aggression in Manchuria in 1931. Asia was too remote for the League to be effective, he believed, and he criticized socialists and pacifists who sought to invoke the League where it "had no power to carry through." Its work was in Europe, Churchill declared. In addition, he expressed sympathy for Japan's position next to Bolshevik Russia and a chaotic China—a view others in Britain shared at the time.[51]

On the other hand, early in the Abyssinian crisis of 1935–1936, Churchill favored strong action against Italy, including sanctions, provided it had wide international backing and was followed through; in this way the League would be strengthened as an agent for rallying opposition against the greater danger of Nazi Germany. But Churchill worried that inaction or a halfhearted policy would undermine the League. He further had misgivings about alienating Italy; doing so would add another front to be defended by the French army, which was naturally preoccupied with Germany, and would also burden Britain's naval position in the Mediterranean. In the event, the government pursued a halfhearted policy, which indeed discredited the League and helped turn Mussolini toward Hitler.[52]

Later, as prime minister, Churchill generally disparaged British planning for a postwar organization to succeed the League, dismissing "these speculative studies" and advising, "'First catch your hare.'" He was more interested in furthering Anglo-American ties and in a Council of Europe, which he saw as a means to contain Russia with the assistance of American power and a revived France. He continued to prefer the regional concept he had advocated in the 1920s.[53]

51. *Speeches*, 5:5219–20.
52. See *WSC* V 652–94 passim, 720, 999.
53. See E. J. Hughes, "Winston Churchill and the Formation of the United Nations Organization," *Contemporary History* 9:4 (1974): 177–94.

In the course of the war, however, Churchill eventually acquiesced in the American desire for a postwar worldwide body, having no choice but to go along with the wishes of his mighty ally. He also likely believed that such a course was the best way to secure American power on behalf of British and European security.

But Churchill wanted to ensure that close ties with America not be jeopardized by the new world organization. With reason he feared the two were seen by some as incompatible. At a dinner with President Roosevelt at Hyde Park in August 1943, he spoke (according to Averell Harriman, who was present) of perpetuating the "fraternal relationship" in peacetime, whereupon Eleanor Roosevelt expressed her fear, as Harriman recorded, that this might "weaken the U.N. concept."[54] One month later, in an address at Harvard, Churchill spoke strongly of the Anglo-American "fraternal association," saying, "whatever form our system of world security may take..., nothing will work soundly or for long without the united effort of the British and American peoples."[55] Churchill's encounter with Mrs. Roosevelt in 1943 was renewed with a more important interlocutor, President Truman, at the Potsdam Conference in July 1945. In his second meeting with Truman, Churchill talked about his hopes for close postwar Anglo-American military cooperation, including continuation of wartime sharing of facilities. Truman agreed, provided, according to Churchill's record of the meeting, that such plans would have to be "fitted in, in some way, as a part of the method of carrying out the policy of the United Nations." Churchill responded that that "was all right so long as the facilities were shared" between just the two of them: "There was nothing in it if they were made common to everybody"; Britain wanted a marriage, not a sibling relationship.[56] Truman's response reflected the Roosevelt policy of cultivating the Russians by avoiding any appearance of Anglo-American collaboration against them, indeed, of posing as mediator between Britain and Russia. Churchill undoubtedly remembered this encounter six months later when he came to draft his Fulton address—with its Anglo-American alliance wrapped in U.N. packaging.

54. W. Averell Harriman and Elie Abel, *Special Envoy to Churchill and Stalin* (New York: Random House, 1975), 222, quoted in *WSC* VII 471.
55. *WSC* VII 493.
56. Harbutt, *Iron Curtain*, 112.

More direct evidence of Churchill's true attitude toward the United Nations is found in his speech to the House of Commons on November 7, 1945, which in retrospect was a preview of Fulton. It included key themes he used four months later: Anglo-American collaboration (stated more bluntly here) and their monopoly of the atomic bomb. But he virtually ignored the United Nations, mentioning it only twice briefly, the second time near the very end of his speech. As the foundation of peace, he instead offered "welcome and salute" to President Truman's "momentous" Navy Day speech of October 27, which, he said, meant the United States "would maintain its vast military power and potentialities, and would join with any like-minded nations, not only to resist but to prevent aggression, no matter from what quarter it came. . . ."[57] Further evidence of Churchill's view is found in a November 1945 letter he sent to the new foreign secretary, Ernest Bevin. He again emphasized the value of sharing British bases with the United States as a means of strengthening their special relationship, which was more important than the United Nations, though it would support the new organization.[58]

Churchill consistently saw first the League and then the United Nations as abstract ideals that were secondary to concrete questions of power and interstate relations. It seems clear that in his Fulton address he used American devotion to the principle of the United Nations to further what he deemed most important, the power relationship between the United States and Britain and the imperative need to block Soviet expansion.

ON ARMS CONTROL

In our world flush with tens of thousands of nuclear weapons, it is difficult to appreciate the depth of feeling among many thoughtful people in 1945–1946 as they saw the idea of apocalypse pass from science fiction into potential reality. No less experienced a figure than the soon-to-be permanent undersecretary at the British foreign office, Sir Orme Sargent, said that "with the arrival of the atomic bomb, civilisa-

57. *Parliamentary Debates*, Commons, 5th ser., vol. 415 (1945), cols. 1290–300 passim.
58. *WSC* VIII 166–67; Harbutt, *Iron Curtain*, 137.

tion was finished. It was merely a question of years—anything, say, from five years to twenty-five years."[59] Similarly, in remarks following Churchill's speech at Fulton, President Truman commented: "We are either headed for complete destruction or are facing the greatest age in history."[60] The same day, the Federal Council of the Churches of Christ condemned the atomic bombings of Japan.[61]

This fear of atomic holocaust and the appalling destruction of the war gave new impetus to the idealist critique of "power politics," and for a time placed international control of atomic weapons at the center of foreign policy debate. The most experienced national security figure in the U.S. government, Secretary of War Henry Stimson, who had had senior responsibility for advising the president on the atomic bomb, took a leading part in advocating international control. On September 12, 1945, and at his final cabinet meeting before retirement, on September 21, Stimson urged that the United States make a "direct approach" to Russia in order to avert an atomic arms race, implicitly (he seems to have been rather vague on essentials) leading to substantial disclosure of atomic secrets. Seven of those present on the twenty-first, including Undersecretary of State Acheson, generally supported his viewpoint.[62] Later, in March 1946, Stimson published a summary of his views in *Harper's*, criticizing "the old pattern of secrecy and sole reliance upon national military superiority" as unsuitable to the atomic revolution. Instead, he advocated "direct and open dealing with other nations" on atomic energy as the only means to "bring us enduring co-operation and an effective community of purpose among the nations of the earth."[63] (In a meeting of the

59. Thomas, *Armed Truce*, 454.
60. *New York Times*, Mar. 6, 1946, 5.
61. *New York Times*, Mar. 6, 1946, 1.
62. See Henry L. Stimson and McGeorge Bundy, *On Active Service in Peace and War* (New York: Harper, 1948), 642–46, for the text of Stimson's memorandum. See also Thomas, *Armed Truce*, 447, and Randall Woods and Howard Jones, *Dawning of the Cold War: The U.S. Quest for World Order* (Athens: University of Georgia Press, 1991), 78–80. For a sympathetic account of Stimson's effort, see McGeorge Bundy, *Danger and Survival* (New York: Random House, 1988), 136–45.
63. Henry L. Stimson, "The Bomb and the Opportunity," *Harper's* (Mar. 1946): 204. "The chief lesson I have learned in a long life is that the only way to make a man trustworthy is to trust him," Stimson wrote, "and the surest way to make him un-

British cabinet in November, some Labour ministers advocated an immediate offer to disclose information to Russia, but were overruled.)[64]

This view was shared by many of the scientists who had worked on the Manhattan Project, sixty-five of whom early in September 1945 had petitioned President Truman to share the secrets of the bomb with other nations.[65] They recognized that the U.S. monopoly would be temporary and were determined to avoid an arms race with Russia; superiority in such weapons was a delusion, they believed.

Taking a more circumspect position, Truman, in an October 3, 1945, message to Congress proposing an Atomic Energy Commission, committed himself generally to the principle of an agreement of the great powers to renounce the bomb and to an exchange of basic scientific information but not engineering know-how.[66] Truman's message was rather vague, however, and, following negative congressional response to reports that the administration was contemplating sharing atomic secrets, he reiterated with more clarity at an impromptu press conference five days later his opposition to any sharing of production secrets.[67] Greatly concerned about the prospect of an atomic arms race, Prime Minister Attlee flew to Washington in November to consult with Truman and the Canadian prime minister, Mackenzie King.[68] Congress then began to debate military versus civilian control of atomic energy, negotiations opened with Russia on creating a U.N. body to deal with the problem, and the Acheson-Lilienthal group started to formulate U.S. policy on international control.

In the midst of what many saw as an apocalyptic debate, Churchill reaffirmed the age-old principles of power politics. Stimson, Acheson, the Manhattan Project scientists, Norman Cousins, and many others saw mankind at a crucial juncture, with atomic weapons requiring a

---

trustworthy is to distrust him and show your distrust." This hardly seemed a wise basis on which to conduct relations with Stalin, and Truman did not follow it.

64. Thomas, *Armed Truce*, 455.

65. Richard G. Hewlett and Oscar E. Anderson Jr., *A History of the United States Atomic Energy Commission*, 2 vols. (University Park: Pennsylvania State University Press, 1962), 1:423.

66. *Truman Papers*, 156.

67. *Truman Papers*, 164.

68. Woods and Jones, *Dawning of the Cold War*, 79–80.

transcendence of history and power politics, which had to be replaced by a new world of cooperation and law. But Churchill, more
impressed with the continuities of human nature and politics, never
shuddered from hard reality. "We all desire to see peace established,"
he observed in 1933. "The differences...arise when our well-meant
sentiments come into contact with extremely baffling and extremely
obstinate concrete obstacles."[69] He believed the danger to peace,
even in the atomic age, lay in departing from power politics; it was
not power politics that had brought on the war, but the West's failure to practice it wisely.

Arms control was nothing new to Churchill. He had endorsed the
1922 Washington Naval Treaty's limits on the number and size of
battleships, as it preserved British superiority over everyone except
the United States and "these comparatively few monsters alone lend
themselves to accurate definition and limitation."[70] He denounced
the 1930 London Naval Treaty, however, which imposed quantitative and qualitative limits on the five main powers' cruisers and de-
stroyers, and quantitative limits on submarines. He believed the
provision for parity between Britain and the United States in practice
meant British inferiority due to her greater needs as an island trading
nation; the treaty limits also weakened her vis-à-vis Japan (whose 70
percent ratio relative to Britain or America's numbers amounted to
de facto Japanese superiority in the Pacific) and would hinder technical development.[71]

The Geneva Disarmament Conference also aroused Churchill's
hostility. In June 1931 he said arms would be reduced not by "artificial agreements" but by "the pressure of expense in hard times, the
growing confidence which comes from a long peace, and the removal of specific [that is, political] causes of danger...." He complained that the one result of the disarmament movement had been
British disarmament, and that Britain had lost her "freedom of design and...power of initiation" in building the fleet. He also criticized "artificial treaty ships" built to satisfy legal terms rather than

69. *Parliamentary Debates*, Commons, 5th ser., vol. 276 (1933), col. 539.
70. *WSC* V C (1) 1032.
71. *Parliamentary Debates*, Commons, 5th ser., vol. 238 (1930), cols. 2096–114
passim.

security needs. "England's hour of weakness," he warned, "is Europe's hour of danger."[72] The London and Washington treaties had a direct impact on the fighting power of the Royal Navy and the United States Navy during the early years of the Second World War, leading to the deaths of many British and American seamen.

Where the disarmament proponents believed arms caused wars, Churchill believed the opposite. "If you wish for Disarmament," he said in May 1932, "it will be necessary to go to the political and economic causes which lie behind the maintaining of armies and navies." Where the National government in its "pious labours" at the Geneva conference was advocating rationalistic solutions based on abstract principles such as equality between France and Germany (which would have required major French reductions and allowed German increases), Churchill focused on the underlying power equation and concrete security needs. In the same speech (eight months before Hitler came to power) he argued:

> I should very much regret to see any approximation in military strength between Germany and France. Those who speak of that as though it were right, or even a mere question of fair dealing, altogether underrate the gravity of the European situation.... For my part, I earnestly hope that no such approximation will take place during my lifetime or in that of my children.... I am sure that the thesis that [Germany] should be placed in an equal military position to France is one which, if it ever emerged in practice, would bring us to within practical distance of almost measureless calamity.

Churchill wanted to "see the foundation of European peace raised upon a more moral basis," but warned, "I am very anxious that the present foundation should not be deranged until...we have built up something satisfactory in its place."[73]

The measureless calamity of World War II could only have deepened Churchill's suspicions of abstract utopianism. Though he supported general disarmament proposals during his second government from 1951 to 1955, out of office, in 1957, he wrote: "I make no plea

72. *Parliamentary Debates*, Commons, 5th ser., vol. 254 (1931), cols. 955–66 passim.

73. *Parliamentary Debates*, Commons, 5th ser., vol. 265 (1932), cols. 2352–53.

for disarmament. Disarmament is a consequence and a manifestation of free intercourse between free peoples."[74]

Churchill's philosophy was to be powerfully vindicated by subsequent events, for arms control, which many in the 1970s and 1980s placed at the heart of East-West relations, had at best a tangential connection to the end of the cold war. The improvement in U.S.-Soviet relations in the later 1980s was achieved in the absence of any strategic arms treaty (START I was signed in July 1991). Negotiations on the two major treaties signed before START—on intermediate-range nuclear missiles (INF) and conventional forces in Europe—had continued for many years without success.

Far more important for the improvement in relations was what Churchill in 1931 called the "pressure of expense in hard times," that is, the economic crisis and resultant political change inside Soviet Russia, in which rising nationalism among the subject peoples of the Soviet Empire also played a major role. That crisis and change were exacerbated by the Reagan military buildup, Russian fears of the Strategic Defense Initiative, and the successful deployment of U.S. INF forces in Europe—in short, by superior power that resulted in the West's victory. This victory strongly confirms Churchill's wisdom: reliance on traditional instruments of superior national power; skepticism of legalistic agreements to ensure security; and an emphasis on underlying political and economic change to reduce armaments, not the other way around.[75]

---

74. Churchill, *The Second World War*, 1-vol. abridgment, 1008.

75. Churchill's critique of disarmament has a direct bearing on the current debate over whether the United States should construct a national missile defense (as distinguished from tactical defenses of troops or of limited areas). Like Churchill and other arms control critics of the 1920s and '30s, today's proponents of missile defense proceed from philosophic assumptions that recognize power as the arbiter of relations between states. Opponents of missile defense, like their forebears whom Churchill challenged, base their position on the old faith in legalistic formulas and sweet reason, as embodied in the now-outdated 1972 Anti-Ballistic Missile Treaty between the United States and Soviet Russia; this agreement sharply limits national missile defenses of the two parties. Despite the growing threat from China and from renegade states such as North Korea, Iraq, and Iran, none of whom is a signatory to the agreement, opponents of missile defense, who direct the policy of the Clinton administration, continue to worship at the altar of a treaty that was negotiated in an entirely different strategic environment; indeed, they have tried to tighten it as part of a

## ON POWER AND PEACE

Churchill's stress on power as the source of peace and security fell harshly on the ears of many Americans, who had been listening to the softer, more idealistic language of Roosevelt and, initially, Truman. Where his critics looked to the United Nations to usher in a new world of cooperation, Churchill advocated a settlement based on superior power.

Power and mercy—"the finest combination in the world," he said in 1919,[76] recalling the words of Macaulay—was one of the main themes of Churchill's public life. Indeed, in his maiden speech to the House of Commons in 1901, at the age of twenty-six, he said that British policy "ought to be to make it easy and honourable for the Boers to surrender, and painful and perilous for them to continue in the field."[77] In 1936 he said, "The whole history of the world is summed up in the fact that when nations are strong they are not always just, and when they wish to be just they are often no longer strong.... Let us have this blessed union of power and of justice."[78]

But superior power was the sine qua non of a peaceful settlement. In 1912 and 1913, as first lord of the admiralty, Churchill proposed a naval holiday, or freeze, in construction of capital ships as a means of controlling the naval race with imperial Germany. This would have

---

broad arms-control agenda encompassing an unverifiable chemical-weapons treaty (now ratified) and a comprehensive nuclear-test ban. Further, officials, both today and during previous administrations, have limited research in and development of missile defenses in obeisance to the dictates of that treaty. They appear to be wholly ignorant of the disastrous history of arms control in the twentieth century; they will not permit hard experience to intrude on their utopian theories. Churchill, in the June 1931 speech attacking the London Naval Treaty quoted in the text, recognized the precise problem that today is hindering development of a national missile defense to protect the American people and our allies: "We have lost our freedom of design and all that power of initiation in which we were the leaders of the world. We are being condemned to building a long series of artificial treaty ships, ships not built to conform to the highest conception of naval architecture for war purposes, but to fit in with the clauses and limitations of Treaties.... The worst feature that has followed from this policy of endeavouring to regulate armaments by means of artificial agreements and conventions has been that we have become so involved in Treaty specifications that we no longer study the naval problem with that precision and intensity which it requires" (*Parliamentary Debates*, Commons, 5th ser., vol. 254 [1931], col. 958).

76. *Parliamentary Debates*, Commons, 5th ser., vol. 113 (1919), col. 85.
77. *Parliamentary Debates*, Commons, 4th ser., vol. 89 (1901), col. 411.
78. *Parliamentary Debates*, Commons, 5th ser., vol. 310 (1936), col. 1530.

preserved Britain's sixteen-to-ten advantage in these vessels. The naval race was unfortunate, but losing Britain's edge would be worse. It was "an appeal of strength striding on in front," he said.[79] The Germans refused.

Churchill applied this principle often in his career. As secretary of state for war in 1920, he favored negotiations with the Irish nationalists, but not under duress. First he wanted to defeat them, saying that "it was necessary to raise the temperature of the conflict to a real issue...and trial of strength...in the hope that there would then be a chance of settlement on wider lines."[80] As chancellor of the exchequer in 1926, he favored concessions to the striking coal miners, but in the subsequent general strike he took a very tough line until the wider stoppage had been broken.[81] This belligerent approach often masked his underlying moderation, but was a serious liability during his career.[82]

In Churchill's view, if two rivals were near equality, then each might think it had a chance of winning. Overwhelming superiority, beyond strict defense needs, was necessary to deter an aggressor: "Margins of naval strength which are sufficient when the time comes to compel a victory, are insufficient to maintain a peace," he told the House of Commons in 1913.[83] In 1932 he criticized disarmament proposals aimed at reducing France's military superiority over Germany: "I say quite frankly, though I may shock the House, that I would rather see another ten or twenty years of one-sided armed peace than see a war between equally well-matched Powers...."[84] And in 1934 he advised the House: "If you want to stop war, you

79. *Parliamentary Debates*, Commons, 5th ser., vol. 50 (1913), col. 1758.
80. Quoted in *WSC* IV 457. At this time Churchill supported the "unofficial" reprisals of the "Black and Tans" against the murders and violence of Sinn Fein. He also favored the use of air power against the rebels (*WSC* IV 455–71).
81. See *WSC* V 146–221.
82. I am grateful to Professor Paul Addison for the point about Churchill's belligerency.
83. *Parliamentary Debates*, Commons, 5th ser., vol. 50 (1913), col. 1790. See also note 6 above. In his March 1936 speech quoted there, Churchill said, "If you are going to run this thing on a narrow margin...you are going to have war. But if you get five or ten to one on one side [with the League], then...you have an opportunity of making a settlement which will heal the wounds of the world" (*Parliamentary Debates*, Commons, 5th ser., vol. 310 [1936], col. 1530).
84. *Parliamentary Debates*, Commons, 5th ser., vol. 272 (1932), col. 88.

gather such an aggregation of force on one side that the aggressor... will not dare to challenge."[85]

The atomic age did not change Churchill's view, which he advocated at Fulton and beyond. In October 1947 he told the Al Smith dinner in New York that it would be all right if Russia left the United Nations so long as the West retained superiority (with the atomic bomb): "Great wars come when both sides believe they are more or less equal, when each thinks it has a good chance of victory."[86]

Churchill was not deflected by the growing fearsomeness of the cold war. He gave this advice in March 1949 on negotiating with communists: "You have not only to convince the Soviet Government that... they are confronted by superior force but that you are not restrained by any moral consideration if the case arose from using that force with complete material ruthlessness." But superiority was a means to a noble end, for in it lay "the greatest chance of peace.... Then the Communists will make a bargain...."[87] Churchill's call at Fulton for a "settlement" was not mere window dressing but was consistent with a formula he had applied for decades and would continue to apply.

To reach a settlement, Churchill made a "summit" the overriding goal of his second administration from 1951 to 1955. In this ambition he was impelled by the growing menace of nuclear weapons and the intensity of the cold war—and perhaps by Labour election campaign charges that he was a "warmonger." He believed the West would now be negotiating from the position of strength it had established since Fulton—with the formation of NATO, for example. (The West did not possess total superiority, however, since Russia maintained vastly bigger land forces and had entered the atomic club in 1949; in truth, Churchill's hopes for a settlement at this time may have been the product of some utopian illusions of his own.) Yet, despite his new emphasis on negotiation, he never abandoned his insistence on power as the means to peace.[88] Thus, in April 1954, which

85. *Parliamentary Debates*, Commons, 5th ser., vol. 292 (1934), col. 731.
86. *Speeches*, 7:7539.
87. *Speeches*, 7:7799.
88. Churchill introduced this use of the word *summit* in his election address in Edinburgh on Feb. 14, 1950 (*Speeches*, 8:7944). For the policy of Churchill's second government, see John W. Young, *Winston Churchill's Last Campaign: Britain and the Cold War, 1951–1955* (Oxford: Clarendon Press, 1996).

was a time of great public anxiety following disclosure of the far greater destructive power and radioactive fallout of the new American hydrogen bomb, he said that U.S. testing "increases the chances of world peace far more than the chances of world war."[89]

Churchill's last great speech was on the subject of nuclear weapons, to a hushed and packed House of Commons on March 1, 1955, at age eighty, one month before his retirement as prime minister. Disarmament would be the best defense, Churchill said, but "'facts are stubborn things.'" In the absence of such an agreement, the "only...sane policy for the free world...is what we call defence through deterrents." He then went on to discuss deterrence in terms of preventing an attack on the British Isles, including a surprise attack: "American superiority in nuclear weapons, reinforced by Britain, must, therefore, be so organised as to make it clear that no such surprise attack would prevent immediate retaliation on a far larger scale.... Not only must the nuclear superiority of the Western Powers be stimulated in every possible way, but their means of delivery of bombs must be expanded, improved and varied."[90] Peace, not only through strength but also through superiority, was the message Churchill had preached throughout his life.[91]

## A Conflict of Visions [92]

In a speech to 17,500 students and others, including veterans, in the Orange Bowl at the University of Miami a week before Fulton, Churchill advised: "Knowledge of the past is the only foundation we have from which to peer into and try to measure the future. Expert knowledge, however indispensable, is no substitute for a generous

89. *Parliamentary Debates*, Commons, 5th ser., vol. 526 (1954), col. 44.
90. *Parliamentary Debates*, Commons, 5th ser., vol. 537 (1955), cols. 1893–905.
91. Churchill did, however, narrow the Royal Navy's margin of superiority when as chancellor of the exchequer from 1924 to 1929 he earnestly enforced the ten-year rule to limit construction of new warships. This rule, established after the Treaty of Versailles, was a planning guideline that assumed there would be no major war for ten years. It was extended each year until Japanese expansion led to its abolition in 1932. See *WSC* V 68–69, 128–30, 288–92; see also 769.
92. See Thomas Sowell, *A Conflict of Visions* (New York: William Morrow, 1987).

and comprehending outlook upon the human story with all its sadness and with all its unquenchable hope."[93] Churchill often wrote of the progress and triumph of liberal ideas, but he was ever mindful of the unavoidable disappointments attendant upon human effort. Thus, in *The River War*, his account of the 1898 Sudan campaign, he had written that "the atmosphere of the earth seems fatal to the noble aspirations of its peoples.... The best efforts of men, however glorious their early results, have dismal endings... [but] the hope strengthens that the rise and fall of men and their movements are only the changing foliage of the ever-growing tree of life, while underneath a greater evolution goes on continually."[94]

Churchill's tragic, but not despairing, view of human capacities rested on his understanding of the concrete experience of history; he was skeptical of abstract reason and its claims for man's supreme ability to remake the world. He agreed with Milton:

> But apt the Mind or Fancy is to rove
> Uncheckt, and of her roving is no end;
> Till warn'd, or by experience taught, she learn
> That not to know at large of things remote
> From use, obscure and subtle, but to know
> That which before us lies in daily life,
> Is the prime Wisdom; what is more, is fume,
> Or emptiness, or fond impertinence,
> And renders us in things that most concern
> Unpractic'd, unprepar'd, and still to seek.[95]

This emphasis on the facts of "daily life" has implications for political change. Writing in 1920, George Santayana criticized "absolute liberty"—the view that man has the capacity to transcend his circumstances and reconstruct society according to utopian ideals of pure reason—as "a foolish challenge thrown by a new-born insect buzzing against the universe." He believed "adaptation to the world at large, where so much is hidden and unintelligible, is only possible piecemeal, by groping with a genuine indetermination in one's

93. *Speeches,* 7:7285.
94. Winston S. Churchill, *The River War* (New York: Award Books, 1964), 45.
95. *Paradise Lost* 8.188–97.

aims." Accordingly, he found "English liberty" superior because it is "vague" and involves "perpetual compromise."[96]

English liberty rests on the common law and the unwritten constitution, whose evolutionary development through practical experience, as distinguished from the articulated reason of individuals, proved the wisdom of this philosophy. The growth of English liberty was examined in the seventeenth century by figures such as Chief Justice Sir Matthew Hale and Sir Edward Coke.[97] Their emphasis on prescriptive facts and a skeptical view of man's nature helped form the basis of the Scottish Enlightenment. Philosophers such as David Hume, Adam Smith, and, later, Edmund Burke viewed society as a plant that changes slowly by natural process, not as a machine that can be altered by the application of pure reason.

Churchill, himself an English historian and aristocrat, was imbued with this philosophy, which lay behind his critique of communism; it defined the political system that he inherited and revered. Churchill agreed strongly with Burke's view of radical change most famously set forth in his denunciation of the leaders of the French Revolution, who saw their country "as nothing but *carte blanche*." A "good patriot," Burke wrote, "always considers how he shall make the most of the existing materials of his country. A disposition to preserve, and an ability to improve," should be the standard of a statesman.[98]

Churchill's originality lay in how he applied Burke's thinking on change and limits to international society. Thus, in March 1936 he described to Conservative M.P.'s Britain's four-hundred-year-old policy of opposition to one-power hegemony in Europe as "the wonderful unconscious tradition of British foreign policy." "I know of nothing that has happened to human nature," he remarked, "which in the slightest degree alters the validity of [our ancestors'] conclusions."[99]

Churchill worked with the "existing materials" of international

96. George Santayana, *Character and Opinion in the United States* (New Brunswick, N.J.: Transaction Publishers, 1991), 228, 200, quoted in Roger Kimball, "Francis Fukuyama on History," *New Criterion* 10:6 (Feb. 1992): 15.

97. See J. G. A. Pocock, "Burke and the Ancient Constitution: A Problem in the History of Ideas," *Historical Journal* 3:2 (1960): 125–43.

98. Edmund Burke, *Reflections on the Revolution in France* (Garden City, N.Y.: Doubleday, 1961), 172.

99. *Speeches*, 6:5694.

society. He recognized from experience and history that power was the arbiter of relations between nations; he desired peace but, reasoning from the facts of daily life, refused to indulge flights of utopianism. He always insisted on facing up to "the cruel and terrible facts" of international life.[100]

Churchill's philosophy was challenged by his utopian critics who, like one of their forebears, Thomas Paine, believed that "every age and generation must be free to act for itself. . . ."[101] Undeterred by Woodrow Wilson's failure a quarter century earlier, they had no doubt that they possessed the wisdom to reconstruct world politics, which, with the advent of atomic weapons, they saw as an absolute necessity.

The two visions came face-to-face in May 1944, when the revered Danish physicist Niels Bohr met with Churchill to urge the necessity of postwar international control of atomic energy and wartime disclosure to Russia of work on the bomb. Bohr believed these policies were vital in order to avert a nuclear arms race that could end in catastrophe. But the meeting was a "disaster," wrote Martin Sherwin in *A World Destroyed*. Sherwin commented on Bohr's motive:

> Bohr believed that under the threat of a nuclear arms race, creative statesmanship—diplomacy based on the possibility of a new and more hopeful future rather than on lessons from the past—could bring the great powers into harmony. There were no historical precedents to encourage him, but the lack of precedent seemed irrelevant—the threat of atomic warfare was also unprecedented. What was necessary, he once remarked to [J. Robert] Oppenheimer in jest, referring to the quantum theory, was "another experimental arrangement."[102]

This underlying approach explains precisely why Churchill barely listened to him.[103]

100. *Parliamentary Debates*, Commons, 5th ser., vol. 113 (1919), col. 182.

101. Thomas Paine, *The Rights of Man* (Garden City, N.Y.: Doubleday, 1961), 277.

102. Martin J. Sherwin, *A World Destroyed* (New York: Alfred A. Knopf, 1975), 107, 95.

103. I do not accept the allegation that Bohr, Szilard, Oppenheimer, or Enrico Fermi turned over atomic secrets to Soviet intelligence, as set forth in Pavel Sudoplatov and Anatolii Sudoplatov with Jerrold L. Schecter and Leona P. Schecter, *Special Tasks: The Memoirs of an Unwanted Witness—A Soviet Spymaster* (Boston: Little,

The conflict of visions is also perfectly captured by comparing Churchill's view on atomic weapons with an article published in spring 1947 by Leo Szilard, a brilliant physicist and veteran of the Manhattan Project, in the recently launched *Bulletin of the Atomic Scientists.* Szilard began his article, "Calling for a Crusade," by noting that, as a scientist, he was "not particularly qualified to speak about the problem of peace." He proceeded anyway because "no one seems to know very much about it." He professed to be mindful of practical obstacles, but then continued at length with a proposal for "permanent peace." He advocated world agencies that, among other things, would build up "a vast consumers' goods industry in a number of countries including Russia" and would arrange improved access to information by assigning a page of the *New York Times* to *Pravda* and vice versa.[104]

Like their successors in our time among scientists and utopians who passionately supported the nuclear freeze of the mid-1980s — and who today resolutely oppose strategic missile defense, despite the growing proliferation threat — Bohr and Szilard could not accept that there might not be a rationalistic solution to the dilemma of a nuclear world of independent nation-states. Fearful of the nuclear danger (and perhaps feeling guilty over their role in creating this new Frankenstein monster), they seriously slighted the inspection and other obstacles posed by the Stalin regime in particular — hardly rational for men of science.[105] They shied away from the "ex-

---

Brown, 1994), 172–220. For rebuttal of this book's claims, see the articles by David Holloway, Vladislav Zubok, and Yuri N. Smirnov in Woodrow Wilson International Center for Scholars, *Cold War International History Project Bulletin* 4 (fall 1994): 50–57. Bohr explained his views in a meeting with President Roosevelt in August 1944. But Roosevelt decided to reject Bohr's advice, for when he met with Churchill at Hyde Park in September, the two leaders agreed not to divulge the atomic bomb project; they also agreed to investigate Bohr's activities. See Sherwin, *A World Destroyed*, 110; Bundy, *On Active Service*, 110–17. Churchill on several occasions rejected the advice of his own scientific advisers who favored Bohr's position, and in September 1945 he strongly objected to a draft proposal by Attlee that took an apocalyptic view of the atomic danger and, on that basis, suggested that the United States share secrets with Russia (Bundy, *On Active Service*, 116, 152).

104. Leo Szilard, "Calling for a Crusade," *Bulletin of the Atomic Scientists* 3:4–5 (Apr.–May 1947): 102–6, 125. The article was subsequently republished in the *Saturday Review.*

105. Bohr and Szilard—and their successors today—exemplify what Hans Morgenthau called "the tragedy of scientific man," who does not understand Herodotus's lament: "Of all the sorrows that afflict mankind, the bitterest is this, that one should

isting materials" of world politics and the "extremely baffling and extremely obstinate concrete obstacles" that Churchill faced up to and put to advantage.[106] They also lacked Churchill's prudent insistence "that the present foundation [of security] should not be deranged until...we have built up something satisfactory in its place."[107]

Their errors and, indeed, their profound and dangerous ignorance of power realities have now been conclusively proved with the opening of some Soviet archives, which demonstrate and confirm the extent of Soviet atomic research and highly successful espionage (led by Klaus Fuchs and the Rosenbergs) by the summer of 1945. One of the leading scholars on this subject, David Holloway, has concluded that Stalin "would still have wanted a bomb" of his own even if Bohr's advice to inform him in advance had been followed. Holloway regards Bohr's view as thoroughly unrealistic.[108]

------

have consciousness of much, but control over nothing." "Fate," Morgenthau wrote, "by giving man the experience of his powers through reason," has allowed "the old *hybris*" to reappear "in the new vestments of a scientific age...." Scientific man "hunts for security where there is none." By contrast, Morgenthau praised the statesman, who achieves "the wisdom by which insecurity is understood and sometimes mastered...." This "is the fulfillment of human possibilities" (*Scientific Man vs. Power Politics* [Chicago: University of Chicago Press, 1946], 188–89). Churchill was such a statesman. In this connection, the reader should recall Churchill's comments on "expert knowledge" at the Orange Bowl. This question was on Churchill's mind, for three months earlier, in a speech to the House of Commons, he had warned scientists against divulging atomic secrets. "Mr. Gladstone said that expert knowledge is limited knowledge," Churchill noted. "On many occasions in the past we have seen attempts to rule the world by experts of one kind or another. There have been theocratic Governments, military Governments and aristocratic Governments. It is now suggested that we should have scientistic—not scientific—Governments" (*Parliamentary Debates*, Commons, 5th ser., vol. 415 [1945], col. 1297). For more on Churchill and "expert knowledge," see the discussion above on his comments about the fall of communism.

106. See note note 98 and then note 69 to this chapter.
107. See note 73 to this chapter.
108. David Holloway, *Stalin and the Bomb* (New Haven: Yale University Press, 1994), 133. Soviet documents show that Klaus Fuchs, who at Los Alamos was "at the center of the work" on design of the atomic bomb, provided data that, in the words of the chief Soviet scientist on their atomic bomb project, was "exceptionally important." Holloway notes that in June 1945 Fuchs "provided a detailed description of the plutonium bomb" and that the first Soviet bomb was "a copy of the American design" (107–8, 138). In addition, any idea of an alternative course to the one pursued by the Truman administration and advocated by Churchill runs up against the untrustworthy figure of Stalin, the man who murdered more people than even Hitler. Yet more evidence that the Russians were already stealing the bomb secrets anyway is found in Harvey Klehr, John Earl Haynes, and Fridrikh Igorevich Firsov, *The Secret World of American Communism* (New Haven: Yale University Press, 1995). With documents

## *Conclusion*

The danger that gripped Bohr, Szilard, and so many others has been greatly reduced, but not by their rationalistic utopian schemes. In truth, the "natural forces" noted by Churchill in 1957 and decades earlier, which worked to "fertilise and vary the thoughts and the power of individual men and women" and to foster the growth of human society "in many forms not comprehended by a party machine," were decisive for the astounding events of 1989–1991. Also decisive were the spiritual and power forces he invoked at Fulton: the "title deeds of freedom" that were "the message of the British and American peoples to mankind"; the "expansion of material well-being" in the free world into "an age of plenty" (to which one may add their immense technological advances); a "new unity in Europe," encompassing a democratized Germany; and the military (including nuclear) strength of the West, led by the English-speaking peoples, who applied wisely history's teachings about power, which they learned at such terrible cost in the 1939–1945 war. Szilard was quite mistaken when he wrote that "no one seems to know very much" about the problem of peace.

---

from the KGB archive, this book shows that the Communist Party of the United States, through its secret apparatus, was working directly with Soviet intelligence to steal U.S. atomic secrets. A "massive amount of high-quality technical intelligence" was obtained on the Manhattan Project, say the authors, which allowed the Soviet project "to proceed much faster and at much lower cost than would otherwise have been possible" (224–25). This massive espionage makes utter nonsense of the utopian views of Bohr and his colleagues and, for that matter, of Stimson. If they had had Churchill's understanding of politics, they would not have pursued their exceedingly naive ideas. Further evidence of widespread Soviet espionage in the United States at this time is found in Harvey Klehr, John Earl Haynes, and Kyrill M. Anderson, *The Soviet World of American Communism* (New Haven: Yale University Press, 1998), and Allen Weinstein and Alexander Vassiliev, *The Haunted Wood: Soviet Espionage in America—The Stalin Era* (New York: Random House, 1998). The best-informed American expert on Russia, George Kennan, shared Churchill's skepticism of the cooperative approach favored by Stimson and the scientists. Kennan wrote in September 1945 that any revelation of vital knowledge without reciprocal guarantees "would constitute a frivolous neglect of the vital interests of our people." Another expert, Thomas Whitney, an attaché at the U.S. embassy in Moscow, emphasized that "the USSR is out to get the atomic bomb" (Bundy, *Danger and Survival,* 178–79). Despite Bundy's earnest effort to find some way that international control might have worked, he concedes: "The notion of an effective control system . . . was absolutely unacceptable to the Soviet Union . . ." (179).

*Five*

⚬ *True Politics and Strategy*

LARRY P. ARNN

The passing of the Soviet menace is a blessing that carries with it also certain problems. It has tended so far to unite liberals in pursuit of a foreign policy that matches what they wish to do at home. It has at the same time sown division in conservative ranks. An anniversary has come that might show us the solution to this problem, if only we will ponder it well.

March 5, 1996, marked the fiftieth anniversary of Winston Churchill's appearance in Fulton, Missouri, to give what became famous as the "Iron Curtain" speech. Even for this man, whose speeches changed the course of the greatest war, here is one of his most consequential utterances. In it he announced the beginning of the cold war and described a policy by which it could be fought. In it he presented a plan for the new world, the world created by the world wars, by the birth of technological conflict, and by the preeminence of American power and principles. We live in that world still today.

We remember the speech most for its bold condemnation of Soviet policy in Eastern Europe: "From Stettin in the Baltic to Trieste in the Adriatic, an iron curtain has descended across the Continent" (8). That was also the part of the speech that received the most dramatic, and the most negative, comment at the time it was given. Recall the background: Britain, led by Churchill, had fought alone against Hitler for a full year after the fall of France; Hitler had attacked the Soviet Union, and Stalin had joined Churchill in the war against Hitler; Churchill, relentlessly wooing a reluctant America, had built with Roosevelt an alliance that became a full war partnership after the attack on Pearl Harbor and Hitler's astonishing declaration of war upon the United States.

These allies won the war. Yet, toward the end strains began to appear in their alliance, strains that became cracks and finally a fissure that separated East from West. In the "Iron Curtain" speech, given less than seven months after the end of hostilities, Churchill declared the separation publicly and made it a recognized fact.

The newspaper reaction in America and most of Europe was negative. In America both the isolationist and the liberal press denounced it, for different reasons. Stalin attacked it bitterly. The Labour government in London was made uncomfortable by strong protests from the socialist rank and file.

Even President Truman kept a public distance from the content of the speech, but that was not the real story. Churchill had warned Truman that an "iron curtain" was being drawn across Europe almost a year earlier, two days after the end of the war in Europe. He had met with Truman to discuss the speech at length on February 10, less than a month before it was given. Truman had also received on February 22 the famous "long cable" from Ambassador George Kennan in Moscow that called for a new American policy toward the Soviet Union. He had traveled to Fulton on a train with Churchill, and he had read the speech and made only approving comments. Then he had stood on the platform and introduced Churchill in Fulton, an extraordinary fact given that Churchill was by then out of power. Finally, he began immediately after the speech the series of maneuvers that built the postwar foreign policy of the United States. The policies of containment, of American commitment to Europe and other key strategic points, and of the maintenance of a dominant nuclear and conventional defense in peacetime followed naturally from the pronouncement at Fulton.

We cannot understand the importance of the speech without

recalling these events, each a hammer blow that has shaped the world in which we live today. Yet, the greatest significance of the speech does not rest in its relation to these immediate incidents. It is decisively a statement of policy and principle for democratic nations, beset with aggressive modern tyranny, menaced by technological weapons. The speech rises to a place above defense and foreign relations, to that summit "where true politics and strategy are one." We can for this reason learn its highest lessons as well today as we could more than fifty years ago.

## The Message to America

To understand the speech, we must begin with the fact that it was addressed to the American people. "It is a solemn moment for the American Democracy. For with primacy in power is also joined an awe-inspiring accountability to the future" (2). A few days later Churchill would make the startling statement that he had come to us at a time when the United States stood "at the highest point of majesty and power ever attained by any community since the fall of the Roman Empire."[1] America is then greater even than Britain at her peak, greater than any nation in modernity. Her model must be that greatest of empires, Rome.

Yet, the United States, unlike Britain and Rome, had never in peacetime discharged such an obligation as now settled upon her. This was true for two powerful reasons. For most of American history, foreign policy has been a small concern. No invader has been poised on our border to strike when we look away. We were sheltered in our hemisphere, preeminent, unassailable, preoccupied with our own public and private affairs. For this reason we were able to sit out much of both world wars. For this reason we held back from securing the peace after the first war.

Nor was this the only reason. America's principles have indeed a global, or rather a universal, reach. But they are not the kind to lead

1. Churchill's March 15, 1946, speech at the Waldorf=Astoria Hotel, in Randolph S. Churchill, ed., *The Sinews of Peace: Winston S. Churchill's Post-War Speeches* (London: Cassell, 1948), 97.

to empire as it has been known in the past. The United States was born with a statement of rights that belong to every man, in every country, in every time. Those rights define both the scope and the purpose of government. Government exists "to secure these rights"; it derives its "just powers from the consent of the governed." What if the people of an imperial domain withhold or withdraw their consent? How then could an American empire maintain its power in that domain?

Churchill had more cause than any living man to understand the significance of these two characteristics of the American makeup. He had spent much of his life encouraging American leadership in world affairs—encouraging it often in vain, encouraging it often to the derision of his countrymen who said it would not come. He had coaxed and begged America into the war, knowing that American intervention was the only hope, and knowing that it might not come. In a miracle deliverance it had come, and with it had come certain victory. Yet, Churchill himself, who had prayed for that deliverance, found himself by the end of the war fretting when America would not listen to his advice about the prosecution of the war or the peace to follow it. Churchill, half American, had held an unshakable faith in America all his life. By 1946, it was a faith that had weathered many storms of experience.

Churchill came then to Fulton not to denounce the Soviet Union, but rather to praise, and also to guide, the greatest power in the history of the world, excepting perhaps one. It is no exaggeration to say that he conceived this as his highest remaining task in the years left to him.

In order to guide America, Churchill proposed "an over-all strategic concept." He chose one of breathtaking reach: "What then is the over-all strategic concept which we should inscribe today? It is nothing less than the safety and welfare, the freedom and progress, of all the homes and families of all the men and women in all the lands" (2). This language recalls the rhetoric of American internationalism as we know it in the twentieth century. That language, as it first developed here, is concocted from the theories that underlie modern liberalism. The two Democratic presidents who articulated that language brought to foreign policy the same utopian vision, the same bent for engineering the new man, that inspired them in politics at home. Woodrow Wilson led us into a war "to end all wars." Franklin Roosevelt laid out as his war aim a new "Bill of Rights," based upon the acceptance of new "self-evident truths" in the economic realm. Every man would have a living, even if that living must come at the expense of another. The problem of economic want could be solved once and for all, and universally.

How, in contrast, would Churchill achieve "the safety and welfare, the freedom and progress, of all the homes and families of all the men and women in all the lands"?

> I have not yet spoken of poverty and privation which are in many cases the prevailing anxiety. But if the dangers of war and tyranny are removed, there is no doubt that science and co-operation can bring in the next few years, certainly in the next few decades, to the world, newly taught in the sharpening school of war, an expansion of material well-being beyond anything that has yet occurred in human experience.... "There is enough for all. The earth is a generous mother; she will provide in plentiful abundance food for all her children if they will but cultivate her soil in justice and in peace." (5–6)

For Churchill, as for Lincoln before him, equality means "the open field and the fair chance"—not an entitlement to the property of another. The mission of the American empire may well be the "safety and welfare" of all the homes and families in all the lands, but the people who live in those homes will be obliged to win their welfare for themselves. Their mother earth has a generous nature to those who cultivate her soil "in justice and in peace."

What conception of justice can these people, spread "through all the lands," answering to many creeds and codes of law, share with one another? They strive, said Churchill, to "bring the family up in the fear of the Lord, or upon ethical conceptions which often play their potent part" (2). The dictates both of revelation and of reason speak, then, to all of them in some way that is common, and it is upon the basis of these dictates that the "over-all strategic concept" must be pursued.

Here America has preeminence. America is best able to "proclaim in fearless tones" the basis of just government, "the great principles of freedom and the rights of man." The United States is not, Churchill argued, the inventor or the sole inheritor of these principles. They belong to all, but they are the special bequest of the "English-speaking world." They come to us "through Magna Carta, the Bill of Rights, the Habeas Corpus, trial by jury, the English common law. . . ." They find their "most famous expression in the American Declaration of Independence" (5).

This is no new or happenstance reference by Churchill to the document by which America was founded. Of course, that same document effected the greatest loss the British Empire would ever sustain, for it would eventually deprive England of her authority throughout the new world. It would eventually lay the foundation for the greatest modern empire, and that empire would not be Britain. Yet, Churchill, an imperialist of a certain type, celebrated that document at Fulton, and in so doing he continued and extended an argument he had been making from the beginning of his career.

In his one and only Fourth of July speech, given also at the end of a world war, Churchill said in 1918:

> The Declaration of Independence is not only an American document. It follows on the Magna Carta and the Bill of Rights as the third great title-deed on which the liberties of the English-speaking people are founded. By it we lost an Empire, but by it we also preserved an Empire. By applying its principles and learning its lesson we have maintained our communion with the powerful Commonwealths our children have established beyond the seas.

The Declaration sprang from a well that "is here by the banks of the Thames, in this island which is the birthplace and origin of the British and American race."[2] At the same time its reach, as its meaning, is universal: "All this means that the people of any country have the right...to choose or change the character or form of government under which they dwell....Here is the message of the British and American peoples to mankind" (5).

It may seem a deft maneuver to adopt as a source of unity between two countries the document that wrought utter, finally violent

2. Winston S. Churchill, *Complete Speeches, 1897–1963,* ed. Robert Rhodes James, 8 vols. (New York: Chelsea House, 1974), 3:2614.

separation between them. If it was a maneuver, it was an old one, one that Churchill had practiced consistently in British politics at home for more than four decades. He had watched socialism take root in the soil prepared by the British class system. He had seen the remedy in the "equality of rights," which is "the whole basis of our political system." To cultivate this doctrine, to plant it deep in the interests of a broad middle class, to make it flourish in that old soil of English history until it choked out the socialist weed—this was the work of his life. Supporting the British monarchy and Empire as he understood them, still he held no principles incompatible with this task. Like Roosevelt and Wilson, he preached and practiced the same lessons, at home and abroad. Only the lessons were not the same.

## America and the World

This understanding of the rights of man, rooted in the experience of England as the first modern world empire, is essential to understanding what Churchill meant by the United Nations. A champion of the League of Nations, Churchill included reference to a "world organization" in most of his major statements on the future of the world. He did not mean the sorry bureaucracy we have today in New York City where tyrants frolic petty and grand. He meant a thing that would have a definite structure, deriving from a common purpose, led by the great Western powers, and operating in line with the interests of its members as they varied from region to region. The United Nations must not be "merely a cockpit in a Tower of Babel" (3). It must have a common purpose. It must have a common language.

Like most of the themes in this speech, that of the "English-speaking peoples" was born early in Churchill's career and was consistently applied. The power of Britain—a ministate even then compared to the behemoth nations—depends upon her connection with the "children," with the "kith and kin" around the globe in the Commonwealth. This connection reaches much farther than merely the nations who still salute the queen or join in the Commonwealth games. It means those nations who share in the British heritage, either by former political connection or by proved friendship to the ideas that emanate from it.

Consequently, the concept of the "English-speaking peoples" implies a method of organizing the world. From his earliest writing before the turn of the century, Churchill conceived the empire as a force for self-government, in line with the interests of both the nations who had achieved it and those who had still to achieve it. He also saw it as crucial to the power of free nations to resist the encroachments of tyrants into vulnerable points. In 1954, as Dien Bien Phu was falling, Churchill would vainly appeal to Eisenhower to make American commitments in Egypt instead of Vietnam. In the former, he argued, Britain had treaty rights at one of the pivotal points on the globe. The latter was less important and more difficult to defend.

Churchill did not, in the Fulton speech or anywhere else, propose that we "go anywhere, pay any price," to defend either power or principle. "It is not our duty at this time when difficulties are so numerous to interfere forcibly in the internal affairs of countries which we have not conquered in war" (5). He was concerned to understand the dangers, to know what were the places that mattered most, to devise methods of defense and security that were efficient. Throughout his career, Churchill was eloquent on the connection between strategy and frugality.

Churchill dwelled famously in the Fulton speech on the "special relationship" between Britain and the United States. That relationship forms the "crux of what I have travelled here to say. Neither the sure prevention of war, nor the continuous rise of world organization will be gained without what I have called the fraternal association of the English-speaking peoples. This means a special relationship between the British Commonwealth and Empire and the United States" (6). This relationship held the key to giving the United Nations the proper thrust. It required a full cooperation on matters military and economic. It required a close coordination of diplomacy. It required the jealous guarding of the "secret knowledge or experience of the atomic bomb," which at that time was thought to belong only to America, Britain, and Canada. It would be "wrong and imprudent" to trust that knowledge to the United Nations (4).

These friends in the cause of free government, who had demonstrated their ability to practice it, must hold real power and must use that power for good. This advice may now seem dated. Power has arisen in countries all over the world, many of them friendly, and it has declined relatively in Britain. The empire is gone, the Commonwealth more form than substance. Yet, recall the cooperation between Thatcher and Reagan and the massive good it achieved. Consider even now to whom we would turn with confidence in any moment of extreme peril.

## Churchill's Challenge Today

The United States still faces the challenge laid down for it in the "Iron Curtain" speech. Liberals know how they wish to respond to that challenge. They are gladly free of the paradox presented by the Soviet Union, whose socialist vision they admired as they might an overzealous sibling, even as the horrors of that sibling plagued them. That embarrassment removed, they know what to do: the whole nation can be a village, and so can the world. Let us help our neighbors abroad, just as we help them here at home: welfare for the world.

Conservatives, on the other hand, have been divided by the victory we have won. They have not united upon any doctrine of international action, nor even upon the idea that international action is vital. They toy with isolationism; they tinker with protectionism.

They must turn from this and face up to a higher calling, a calling that emanates from the principles that made our nation what it is. If we listen to Churchill, we will follow that calling. We will recall that self-government is an entitlement of all, yet its achievement and sustenance are the highest—and the rarest—political accomplishments. The nations who have it carry a responsibility to the world, and also to themselves and to their posterity. They are right, then, to consult their interests as they do their duty in the world. Duty and interest alike encourage them to shoulder the burden of their own defense and the defense of their cause among men. To do it well, they must have courage and persistence, for the world still presents awful dangers.

They must also cultivate that high prudence that was the Churchill hallmark. He studied the problems of security and foreign policy for a lifetime. He knew them in their full dimension, as elements of politics more generally. A half brother of our country, he is the profoundest student in this century of the American mission in the world. If we are to be worthy of the place we hold, we must learn from him, and soon.

## Six

## Rhetorical Statesmanship

PATRICK J. C. POWERS

As the twentieth century draws to a close, the momentum intensifies to evaluate the distance traversed and the events endured over the last hundred years. Who will emerge in the public stocktaking as having contributed most impressively to the progress of Western civilization and the pursuit of world peace? Surely, *Time,* the grand old journal of democratic public opinion, will announce its man of the century, just as in 1950 it proclaimed the man of the half century. Despite the continuing decline of democratic interest in public affairs, at least one or two political figures will be among the final nominees. As in 1950, when he was named man of the half century, strong arguments will once again favor Winston Churchill's candidacy. As recently as 1996, Churchill's celebrated "Iron Curtain" address, delivered fifty years earlier in Fulton, Missouri, was widely praised for the lessons it provides about the future of Russia after the cold war. Why does the memory of Churchill remain so powerful more than forty years after he left office in 1955, and more than thirty years since he died in 1965? Why should Churchill's influence persist into the twenty-first century?

The evidence supporting the case for honoring Churchill after the turn of the century is as

powerful today as it was at the height of his fame in 1950. His governance of Great Britain during her darkest yet finest hour in the Second World War was the necessary and noble foundation for the
subsequent victory of the Allies over Nazi Germany. Without his
statesmanship, popular support for liberal democracy would not have
survived the war. Forced to confront the Nazis alone, the United
States could very well have retreated into isolationism. A united democratic front would never have formed against the Soviet Union's
spread of communism. Surely, there would have been greater resistance to remembering the Holocaust. One can only imagine how
many atomic weapons might have been used as blackmail or even
dropped. The Western democracies owe their success in prevailing
over the totalitarian regimes to Churchill's statesmanship from the
late thirties through the early fifties.

Churchill's decisive assistance during and after the war in helping
Western democratic regimes avoid political catastrophe is, however,
merely the surface evidence supporting his nomination as statesman
of the century. In the aftermath of the collapse of the Soviet Union
and the restoration of political arrangements prior to the Second
World War, Europe has in some sense been transported back to the
context of politics after the First World War. In the renewed political
atmosphere of a world of sovereign nations freed from abstract and
imperialist ideologies, reconsideration of Churchill's political perspective has once again become timely and relevant to discussions
about the fate of democracy in the next century.

Central to Churchill's political convictions was a preoccupation
with extending the influence of democracy in the modern world.
Persuading the governing representatives of liberal democratic
regimes that the perpetuation of civilization requires the exercise of
statesmanship remained his lifelong concern. Churchill's personal
success at galvanizing the beleaguered English-speaking peoples into
defending themselves against the Nazi and communist threats de-
rived from his belief that modern democratic rulers must lead, as well
as be led by, the will of the people they represent. From the perspective of political principles, the case for praising Churchill as the man of
the twentieth century rests not just on his success during the six years
of World War II but, more important, on the political significance of

his lifelong record of moral leadership in deed and word. Viewed as a whole, his more than sixty years in politics stand as a model of statesmanship worthy of continued admiration and imitation by leaders of democratic regimes.

## *Churchill's Record of Political Failures*

There is something extremely ironic, nonetheless, about the possibility that Churchill might be acknowledged as the most prominent public figure of the last hundred years. Despite the evidence for his pervasive influence in the century's most decisive event, the Second World War, it remains difficult to characterize Churchill as a successful politician. By the mid-1930s, when he was already sixty years old, he was evaluated as a man who had once shown great promise but in the end had amounted to little. He had switched parties twice, something that British politics does not normally tolerate even once. He had proposed constitutional changes to handle the Irish and India situations, as well as the general problems of governing the empire and managing modern economic crises. Yet, these ideas had come to naught. He had a plan for shortening the endless slaughter of World War I: break through the Dardanelles and demoralize the Ottoman Empire into quitting. It failed, the war dragged on, and Churchill resigned with the Dardanelles albatross around his neck thereafter.

Then there were the defeating events at the conclusion of World War II. No sooner had the Germans surrendered than the British cashiered Churchill in the general election of July 1945. With the approach of the war's end, he had anticipated his sacking at the hands of the democratic voters. As news of victory over the Nazis reached England, he commented to General Ismay that "the eagle has ceased to scream, but the parrots will now begin to chatter. The war of the giants is over and the pygmies will now start to squabble." While he was forced to bow to democracy's verdict, he never accepted its judgment. After losing the election, he commented that "surely this was the first time when the winner of the greatest horse race in history had been warned off the course." When younger party colleagues tried to ease him out of the leadership of the Conservative Party and into a grand tour of English cities, he declined with the tart remark that "I refuse to be exhibited like a prize bull whose chief attraction is his past prowess."[1] Even when the Conservative Party was returned to power in 1950, with Churchill restored to the prime ministry, he was no longer considered effective by younger Conservative M.P.'s in combating the damage to national interests wrought by the Labour Party. While his tenure was tolerated as a reward for his exceptional services during the war, it was not viewed as a political success. Although Churchill was the winner of the greatest horse race in history, his victory was preceded and succeeded by a series of incomplete efforts and defeats.

Until recently, democratic citizens of all stripes believed that Churchill's own moral strength endowed the event of World War II with its elevated character. They saw Churchill as the exceptional jockey who inspired the steed of democracy, and whose statesmanship turned the race of World War II into the greatest in history. At the same time, when Churchill's singular success in the war is weighed against his longer record of political nonsuccesses, it is hard to ignore the opinion of some contemporary critics that the event of the Second World War made the man. They view the war as a conflict of such magnitude and majesty that it inspired the horse of British democracy to stretch its limits and thereby carry its lucky rider Churchill into the winner's circle of history.

Even if one disagrees with the dissenters over Churchill's role in wringing victory from near defeat, how can one avoid drawing the conclusion that as belief in the historical importance of World War II fades, so will any continuing influence of Winston Churchill on the twenty-first century? Defending Churchill's political greatness requires questioning the conventional assumption that his enduring political worth depends solely on his record in the Second World War. Appreciating the timeless importance of Churchill's counsel about how and why to advance civilization for all mankind depends on recognizing the eventual benefit to democracy of his recurring political failures. One needs to recover Churchill's awareness that his

1. Kay Halle, *Irrepressible Churchill* (Cleveland: World, 1966), 250–51.

outstanding political achievement of leading Great Britain to victory in World War II was the direct consequence of a lifelong lack of conventional political success in the British parliamentary democratic regime.

## *"The Sinews of Peace" or the "Iron Curtain" Speech*

The fate of Churchill's historic Fulton address about the coming threat of Soviet Russia exemplifies the ironic way in which his rhetorical statesmanship achieved long-term influence, despite its lack of immediate and complete success. At the time, Churchill titled the address "The Sinews of Peace." Since then, it has become famous as the "Iron Curtain" speech. In the distinction between his intention for the title and history's recollection of it lies both the immediate problem and the long-term promise of the exercise of statesmanship in twentieth-century democracies. Churchill's title reflected his concern to unveil a threefold plan for preventing a third world war between the Western democracies and Soviet Russia: to reach an understanding on all points of contention with Russia under the authority of the United Nations Organization; to use the newly founded United Nations Organization to preserve that understanding; and, most important, to employ the "whole strength of the English-speaking world and all its connections" to enforce that understanding (12). When implemented together, these strands or sinews held forth the promise of peace.

Quickly, however, Churchill's "over-all strategic concept" of promoting the "fraternal association of the English-speaking peoples" was neglected (6). Today it is hard to conceive that "British moral and material forces and convictions" (13) will ever become so tightly knit to those of the United States as to achieve the principle of joint citizenship that Churchill believed to be their common destiny. Even more overlooked has been the heart of Churchill's address, namely, his appeal to the political principles justifying "a special relationship between the United States and the British Commonwealth" (7). The British and American peoples had an exceptional obligation, "an awe-inspiring accountability" to the future (2). For centuries, the

English-speaking peoples had been bound by their common belief that "the great principles of freedom and the rights of man" (5) ought to be available to the people of any country. Unlike Woodrow Wilson, Churchill never felt that Western democracies were obligated to make the world safe for democracy. The fraternal democracies must, nonetheless, proclaim fearlessly the message of freedom for all mankind by combining their resources to prevent the spread of war and tyranny. As he said, "Let us preach what we practise—let us practise what we preach" (5). Despite his best efforts, however, Churchill's aspiration for Anglo-American unity remains a dream fifty years after the Fulton address.

Viewed from the long-term perspective, on the other hand, the speech had, and continues to have, lasting and beneficial effects. Popular memory quickly immortalized the section of the address describing the threat posed by Soviet Russia, rather than the solution for peace proposed by Churchill. "From Stettin in the Baltic to Trieste in the Adriatic, an iron curtain has descended across the Continent" (8). These chilling words were the clarion call that galvanized the Western allies, and especially the English-speaking peoples, into recognizing the need for concerted action. Over time, Churchill's rhetorical efforts did succeed in effecting a high degree of common understanding between English and American leaders. On the level of tactics, his plan for constructing a united political and military front against Soviet Russia succeeded tolerably well. Forty years later, democratic leaders such as Thatcher and Reagan would attribute the ultimate fall of communism to the fidelity of Western democracies to the admonitions of Churchill and others about the need to support political principles with military strength.

## The Limitations and Strengths of Democracy

Even as he delivered the Fulton address, Churchill acknowledged that the double-edged weakness and success of his own rhetorical statesmanship was rooted in the limitations and strengths of democracy. He cautioned, as well as praised, the American democracy for having succeeded in ascending to the pinnacle of world power. The

United States should feel not only a sense of having done its duty but also an anxiety lest it fall short of its level of achievement. This mixed account of the United States at the moment of its greatest world power reflected Churchill's lifelong tendency to be of two minds about the worth of democratic government.

As a partisan of Abraham Lincoln's democratic conception of government of the people, by the people, and for the people, Churchill was an advocate of representative government. He knew, of course, that in daily practice the people are accustomed to obey the decisions of Parliament and that the representative rulers are not afraid to use compulsion upon recalcitrants. Yet, in exercising executive authority, the representatives should always legislate and act only in response to the "settled persistent will of the people." They should never look on themselves as a caucus, obtaining a fixed term of office by promises and then doing what it likes with the people. The idea that a handful of people could get hold of the state machinery and assert a right to make the people do what suits their party and personal interests or doctrines, Churchill argued, is antithetical to every conception of modern democracy. Prevailing democratic sentiment, on the contrary, holds that the people should continuously rule and that public opinion expressed by all constitutional means should shape, guide, and control the actions of ministers who are their servants and not their masters.[2]

At the same time, despite his lifelong respect for the principles of equality, liberty, and self-government, Churchill was often less than flattering in his judgments about democracy's actual practice. He never deceived himself into thinking that democracy was a perfect form of government. In 1947, during a speech criticizing the Labour government's Parliament Bill, which would have curbed the authority of the House of Lords to check legislation passed by the House of Commons, Churchill gave voice to his most famous yet ironic praise of democracy: "Many forms of government have been tried—and will be tried in this world of sin and woe. No one pretends that democracy is perfect or all-wise. Indeed, it has been said that democracy is the worst

---

2. Winston S. Churchill, *Complete Speeches, 1897–1963,* ed. Robert Rhodes James, 8 vols. (New York: Chelsea House, 1974), 6:7565–66.

form of government except all those other forms that have been tried from time to time."[3] What is so bad about democracy, and which part is defective? Every part was, in turn, the object of Churchill's critical humor. About the willingness and ability of the elected representatives to serve the settled will of the people, he was often pessimistic. Out of exasperation with the government over the 1927 budget, he characterized democracy as a "government of the duds, by the duds, and for the duds." The people fared no better in his eyes. As early as 1910, during a period of parliamentary supremacy he would later characterize as the golden age of government by eminent men, Churchill took a dim view of the political competence of the electorate. "Under our representative institutions," he said, "it is occasionally necessary to defer to the opinions of other people."[4]

The weaknesses of popular government did not lead Churchill to view democracy as a second-best or compromise form of government. Imperfect democracy does not become attractive merely by default, due to the well-known difficulties of implementing supposedly better forms of government such as aristocracy or enlightened monarchy. On the contrary, Churchill knew from experience that the other political forms are as essentially defective as democracy. By virtue of necessitating the exercise of governmental command in order to secure the common goods of health, honor, and happiness, every political regime is intrinsically flawed. Only in some limited sense is democracy a better form of political order. Because the authority of democratic government derives from the consent of the governed, democracy is infected by a less virulent form of the fundamental flaw of coercion intrinsic to the nature of political life as such. Until the post–World War I era, democracy had flourished under the conditions of modern life. By the 1930s, however, the crisis over the future direction of modern society had triggered a crisis over the survival of democracy as such. Since Churchill conceived of democracy as the best of the worst governmental forms, he understood the far-reaching implications of the dangers confronting

3. Ibid., 7566.
4. Colin Coote, ed., *Maxims and Reflections* (Boston: Houghton Mifflin, 1949), 143; Halle, *Irrepressible Churchill*, 249.

democratic self-government. If the worth of democracy were discredited, there would remain no form of civilized rule on which to fall back. As the increasing strength of Hitler and Stalin had ominously revealed during the thirties, mankind would be unable to resist succumbing to the tyranny of force.

Why was Churchill convinced that parliamentary democracy was the best among the "worst" forms of government? Until recent times, it had been generally accepted that the best way of governing states is by talking.[5] The hallmark of liberal democratic government is the assembly of its representatives in a "parliament" for the purpose of resolving its affairs through direct discussion and argument. As Churchill said in the Fulton address, it was at Westminster, the home of the House of Commons, that he received a large portion of his education in "politics, dialectic, rhetoric, and one or two other things" (1).

Democracy's respect for the political authority of speech is the source for the possible amelioration of its ills. The democratic principle of equality allows all representatives access to the political forum. There they exercise their rhetorical capacities for the sake of persuading citizens about the direction to be adopted by the regime. Reliance on a rhetorical approach to the resolution of political disagreements is particularly appropriate for outstanding democratic leaders who are repeatedly elected by the people to "bear exceptional responsibilities and discharge duties upon a very great scale" over prolonged periods.[6] Such democratic representatives, who possess impressive abilities for sustained reflection and character, are well suited by nature and nurture to influence democratic opinion about how best to secure the common goods of life, liberty, and the pursuit of happiness for all. To be sure, the difficulty of obtaining voluntary agreement among the many opinions characteristic of democratic politics increases the probability that even exceptional democratic statesmen will not succeed in securing quick and easy political solutions. At the same time, the possibility that a democratic citizenry may gradually respond to repeated exhorta-

5. Churchill, *Complete Speeches,* 5:4853.
6. Winston S. Churchill, *Thoughts and Adventures* (New York: Norton, 1991), 216.

tions increases the prospects for some eventual if diluted influence of rhetorical statesmanship over democratic opinion. In light of the fact that a democratic statesman's efforts may never fully achieve the desired results he intends, his effectiveness should not be judged by whether his success has been immediate and complete. Rather, a democratic leader's beneficial effect is best measured by his rhetorical success over time at habituating his constituents to strive to be as faithful as they can to the civilized standards by which a democratic regime aspires to live.

## Churchill's Rhetorical Legacy

The "Iron Curtain" address is striking for Churchill's candor that his political influence depended on his rhetorical abilities. By stressing his status as a private visitor in delivering his remarks—since in 1946 he was no longer prime minister but only leader of the Opposition— Churchill acknowledged his lack of executive authority to implement any proposals for peace. Nonetheless, he availed himself of the freedom permitted every citizen in a democracy, "to give my true and faithful counsel in these anxious and baffling times" (2). Having long since satisfied private ambitions for fame, his only motive in speaking frankly was to do his duty. He reiterated his earlier assertion that the sole authority for his remarks was his belief in what he knew to be the truth about Soviet Russia. As Churchill said, "I speak only for myself." In his case, however, his solitary status carried more weight than it might have for the average democratic citizen. Churchill brought "the experience of a lifetime" in public affairs to bear on "the problems which beset us on the morrow of our absolute victory in arms." By concluding the preamble of his address with a promise to try "with what strength I have" to preserve the democratic gains in World War II, Churchill made clear his conviction about the real source of his or any democratic leader's strength (2). All of Churchill's political power resided in his rhetorical capacity for persuading his audience of the truth about the "shadow [that] has fallen upon the scenes so lately lighted by the Allied victory" (8).

Were Churchill alive today, it would not surprise him that the full

extent of his intentions in the "Iron Curtain" speech had not come
to pass. After his experience during the thirties of crying in the
wilderness over Hitler, he harbored no illusions about overcoming
the recurring difficulty of rousing democracies to vigilance in their
own self-interest. "Last time I saw it all coming and I cried aloud to
my own fellow-countrymen and to the world, but no one paid any
attention" (12). Then, the cause of the problem was simple but re-
calcitrant. The democracies failed to heed his warning that peace is
not self-perpetuating, but needs to be defended. While the opponent
had changed in 1946 from the Nazis to the communists, the blind-
ness of the Western democracies to the threat of tyranny and war
persisted. Yet, there was a difference: in the aftermath of the war,
Churchill could appeal to an awakened, if exhausted, democratic
conscience. Although they failed to listen the last time, democratic
citizens might have finally learned the lesson of their foolish ways.
"We ... surely must not let that happen again. This can only be
achieved by reaching now, in ... 1946, ... a good understanding on all
points with Russia ..." (12). As President Truman's presence on the
podium with the private visitor underscored, this time Churchill
hoped that his rhetorical statesmanship would exercise an authorita-
tive influence over the future direction of democratic foreign policy.
The eventual fall of the Soviet Union and communism confirmed
that his expectations were not entirely misbegotten.

From the start of his political career, Churchill chose to invest his
own exceptional talents as a democratic representative in the enter-
prise of public speech. He never banked his hopes for success as a
leader on mastering the technical expertise required to administer
the public application of scientific progress. Rather, he sought to advance the principles of Western civilization by employing his vast
rhetorical abilities to remind English-speaking citizens of their political responsibilities. Churchill understood that the strength of democratic rhetoric is its utility for informing democratic citizens, charged
with responsibility for choosing their rulers, of the civilized standards
by which to measure the conduct of their representatives. Throughout his career as a statesman, Churchill practiced an exhortative rhetoric aimed at the moral improvement of his democratic constituents.
He did so with the full knowledge that he would not always be of

immediate influence. As Churchill's lifelong recurrent political failures testify, a democratic representative may ostensibly fail to persuade in the short run. Over time, however, he may ultimately prevail, as did Churchill.

At his retirement from the House of Commons, after more than sixty years of public speaking, Churchill's words had arguably done more than the actions of all other public figures in this century to strengthen the resolve and ability of Western civilization to preserve and perfect the possibilities of liberal democracy for posterity. Almost forty years later, Churchill's incisive and persuasive formulations of long-established truths about the beneficial yet precarious character of democratic regimes continue to exert influence. His speeches constitute a rhetorical legacy for contemporary and future politicians who aspire to carry on his efforts at perpetuating the opportunities for liberty and equality afforded by democracy.

The enduring vitality of his exhortations would not have surprised Churchill. In concluding the Fulton address, he said that if his proposals for peace were given due consideration, then "the highroads of the future will be clear, not only for us but for all, not only for our time, but for a century to come" (13). Achievement of such a lasting influence in the popular memory, even if only in the diluted form of a misnomered respect for the "Iron Curtain" speech, was essential to his intention in delivering the address titled "The Sinews of Peace."

As the Western democracies agonize once more, and not for the last time, over how best to establish constructive foreign policies with Russia in the post–cold war era, they could hardly do better than to seek counsel from Churchill. Fifty years ago, he had already thought through the mystery, enigma, and riddle that is Russia. Fifty years from now, should the Western democracies be gifted with the presence of a statesman competent in foreign policy, more likely than not that individual will acknowledge his debt to Churchill. At Fulton, Missouri, in 1946, Winston Churchill delivered a memorable address in which he provided future democratic statesmen with an exemplary and compelling account of a judicious, civilized, and enduring way for the English-speaking peoples to coexist with Mother Russia.

# Epilogue

## New Threats for Old

MARGARET THATCHER

When my distinguished predecessor delivered his Fulton speech, exactly fifty years ago, he journeyed hither by train in the company of the President of the United States. On the way, they played poker to pass the time. And the President won $75—quite a sum in those non-inflationary times for an unemployed former Prime Minister. But in view of the historic impact of his speech on American opinion and subsequently on US foreign policy, Sir Winston Churchill later recorded that his loss was one of the best investments he had ever made.

I did not travel here by train; nor in the company of the President of the United States; nor did I play poker. I don't have the right kind of face for it. But there is some similarity in the circumstances of fifty years ago and today.

Mr. Churchill spoke not long after the Second World War. Towards the end of that great conflict, the wartime allies had forged new international institutions for post-war co-operation. There was in those days great optimism, not least in the United States, about a world without conflict presided over benevolently by bodies like the United Nations, the IMF, the World Bank and the GATT. But the high hopes reposed in them were increasingly disappointed as

151

Stalin lowered the Iron Curtain over Eastern Europe, made no secret of his global ambitions and became antagonist rather than ally. Churchill's speech here was the first serious warning of what was afoot, and it helped to wake up the entire West.

In due course, that speech bore rich fruit in the new institutions forged to strengthen the West against Stalin's assault.

The Marshall Plan laid the foundations for Europe's post-war economic recovery.

The Truman Doctrine made plain that America would resist communist subversion of democracy.[1]

The North Atlantic Treaty Organization mobilized America's allies for mutual defence against the Soviet steamroller.

And the European Coal and Steel Community,[2] devised to help reconcile former European enemies, evolved over time into the European Community.

Stalin had overplayed his hand. By attempting to destroy international co-operation, he succeeded in stimulating it along more realistic lines—and not just through Western "Cold War" institutions like NATO. As the West recovered and united, growing in prosperity and confidence, so it also breathed new life into some of the first set of post-war institutions like the GATT and the IMF. Without the Russians to obstruct them, these bodies helped to usher in what the Marxist historian Eric Hobsbawm[3] has ruefully christened the "Golden Age of Capitalism." The standard of living of ordinary people rose to levels that would have astonished our grandparents; there were regional wars, but no direct clash between the superpowers; and the economic, technological and military superiority of the West eventually reached such a peak that the communist system was forced into first reform, then surrender, and finally liquidation.

None of this, however, was pre-ordained. It happened in large

1. Proposing assistance for Greece and Turkey on March 12, 1947, President Truman said, "I believe it must be the policy of the United States to support free peoples who are resisting attempted subjugation by armed minorities or by outside pressures."

2. The European Coal and Steel Community (ECSC) was established in 1952 by France, Italy, West Germany, Belgium, the Netherlands, and Luxemburg.

3. Eric Hobsbawm (born 1917), British historian. Professor of Economic and Social History at London 1970–1982.

part because of what Churchill said here fifty years ago. He spoke at a watershed: one set of international institutions had shown themselves to be wanting; another had yet to be born. And it was his speech, not the "force" celebrated by Marx, which turned out to be the midwife of history.

Today we are at what could be a similar watershed. The long twilight struggle of the Cold War ended five years ago with complete victory for the West and for the subject peoples of the communist empire—and I very much include the Russian people in that description. It ended amid high hopes of a New World Order. But those hopes have been grievously disappointed. Somalia,[4] Bosnia and the rise of Islamic militancy all point to instability and conflict rather than co-operation and harmony.

The international bodies, in which our hopes were reposed anew after 1989 and 1991, have given us neither prosperity nor security. There is a pervasive anxiety about the drift of events. It remains to be seen whether this generation will respond to these threats with the imagination and courage of Sir Winston, President Truman and the wise men of those years.

## The Post–Cold War World

But, first, how did we get to our present straits?

Like the break-up of all empires, the break-up of the Soviet empire wrought enormous changes way beyond its borders.

Many of these were indisputably for the good:

—a more co-operative superpower relationship between the US and Russia;

—the spread of democracy and civil society in Eastern Europe and the Baltics;

—better prospects for resolving regional conflicts like those in South Africa and the Middle East, once Soviet mischief-making had been removed;

4. U.S. and, later, UN forces intervened in Somalia from December 1992 to March 1995 to protect famine relief from the effects of civil war, but they failed to secure peace and stability.

—the discrediting of socialist economic planning by the exposure of its disastrous consequences in Russia and Eastern Europe;

—and the removal of Soviet obstruction from the United Nations and its agencies.

These were—and still are—real benefits for which we should be grateful.

But in the euphoria which accompanied the Cold War's end—just as in what Churchill's private secretary called "the fatal hiatus" of 1944 to 1946—we failed to notice other, less appealing, consequences of the peace.

Like a giant refrigerator that had finally broken down after years of poor maintenance, the Soviet empire in its collapse released all the ills of ethnic, social and political backwardness which it had frozen in suspended animation for so long:

—suddenly, border disputes between the successor states erupted into small wars in, for instance, Armenia and Georgia;[5]

—within these new countries the ethnic divisions aggravated by Soviet policies of Russification and forced population transfer produced violence, instability and quarrels over citizenship;

—the absence of the legal and customary foundations of a free economy led to a distorted "robber capitalism," one dominated by the combined forces of the mafia and the old communist *nomenklatura*, with little appeal to ordinary people;

—the moral vacuum created by communism in everyday life was filled for some by a revived Orthodox Church, but for others by the rise in crime, corruption, gambling and drug addiction—all contributing to a spreading ethic of luck, a belief that economic life is a zero-sum game, and an irrational nostalgia for a totalitarian order without totalitarian methods;

—and, in these Hobbesian conditions,[6] primitive political ideologies which have been extinct in Western Europe and America for two

5. The conflicts between Armenia and Azerbaijan over Nagorno Karabakh, and between Georgia and the separatist republic of Abkhazia, escalated into wars in 1991 and 1992 respectively. Ceasefires were agreed in 1994, and peace talks and border clashes continue.

6. In *Leviathan* (1651), English philosopher Thomas Hobbes (1588–1679) described the state of nature as an anarchic struggle of each against all.

generations surfaced and flourished, all peddling fantasies of imperial glory to compensate for domestic squalor.

No one can forecast with confidence where this will lead. I believe that it will take long years of civic experience and patient institution-building for Russia to become a normal society. Neo-communists may well return to power in the immediate future, postponing normality; but whoever wins the forthcoming Russian elections[7] will almost certainly institute a more assertive foreign policy, one less friendly to the US.

## New Threats for Old

A revival of Russian power will create new problems—just when the world is struggling to cope with problems which the Soviet collapse has itself created outside the old borders of the USSR.

When Soviet power broke down, so did the control it exercised, however fitfully and irresponsibly, over rogue states like Syria, Iraq and Gadaffi's Libya. They have in effect been released to commit whatever mischief they wish, without bothering to check with their arms supplier and bank manager. Note that Saddam Hussein's invasion of Kuwait took place after the USSR was gravely weakened and had ceased to be Iraq's protector.

The Soviet collapse has also aggravated the single most awesome threat of modern times: the proliferation of weapons of mass destruction. These weapons—and the ability to develop and deliver them—are today acquired by middle-income countries with modest populations such as Iraq, Iran, Libya and Syria—acquired sometimes from other powers like China and North Korea, but most ominously from former Soviet arsenals, or unemployed scientists, or from organized criminal rings, all via a growing international black market.

According to Stephen J. Hadley, formerly President Bush's Assistant Secretary for International Security Policy: "By the end of the decade, we could see over twenty countries with ballistic missiles,

7. Presidential elections were scheduled to be held in Russia on June 16, 1996.

nine with nuclear weapons, ten with biological weapons, and up to thirty with chemical weapons."

According to other official US sources, all of North-East Asia, South-East Asia, much of the Pacific and most of Russia could soon be threatened by the latest North Korean missiles. Once they are available in the Middle East and North Africa, all the capitals of Europe will be within target range; and on present trends a direct threat to American shores is likely to mature early in the next century.

Add weapons of mass destruction to rogue states, and you have a highly toxic compound. As the CIA has pointed out: "Of the nations that have or are acquiring weapons of mass destruction, many are led by megalomaniacs and strongmen of proven inhumanity or by weak, unstable or illegitimate Governments." In some instances, the potential capabilities at the command of these unpredictable figures are either equal to—or even more destructive than—the Soviet threat to the West in the 1960s. It is that serious.

Indeed, it is even more serious than that. We in the West may have to deal with a number of possible adversaries, each with different characteristics. In some cases their mentalities differ from ours even more than did those of our old Cold War enemy. So the potential for misunderstanding is great, and we must therefore be very clear in our own minds about our strategic intentions, and just as clear in signalling these to potential aggressors.

And that is only the gravest threat. There are others.

Within the Islamic world the Soviet collapse undermined the legitimacy of radical secular regimes and gave an impetus to the rise of radical Islam. Radical Islamist movements now constitute a major revolutionary threat not only to the Saddams and Assads[8] but also to conservative Arab regimes, who are allies of the West. Indeed they challenge the very idea of a Western economic presence. Hence the random acts of violence designed to drive American companies and tourists out of the Islamic world.

In short, the world remains a very dangerous place, indeed one menaced by more unstable and complex threats than a decade ago.

8. General Hafiz Assad (born 1930), Syrian politician. Secretary of the Ba'ath Party 1970– ; President of Syria 1971– ; Commander-in-Chief 1973– .

But because the risk of total nuclear annihilation has been removed, we in the West have lapsed into an alarming complacency about the risks that remain. We have run down our defences and relaxed our guard. And to comfort ourselves that we were doing the right thing, we have increasingly placed our trust in international institutions to safeguard our future. But international bodies have not generally performed well. Indeed, we have learned that they cannot perform well unless we refrain from utopian aims, give them practical tasks, and provide them with the means and backing to carry them out.

## *Institutional Failure*

### THE UNITED NATIONS

Perhaps the best example of utopian aims is multilateralism; this is the doctrine that international actions are most justified when they are untainted by the national interests of the countries which are called upon to carry them out. Multilateralism briefly became the doctrine of several Western powers in the early nineties, when the United Nations Security Council was no longer hamstrung by the Soviet veto. It seemed to promise a new age in which the UN would act as world policeman to settle regional conflicts.

Of course, there was always a fair amount of hypocrisy embedded in multilateralist doctrine. The Haiti intervention by US forces acting under a United Nations mandate,[9] for instance, was defended as an exercise in restoring a Haitian democracy that had never existed; but it might be better described, in the language of Clausewitz,[10] as the continuation of American immigration control by other means. But honest multilateralism without the spur of national interest has led to intervention without clear aims.

No one could criticize the humane impulse to step in and relieve the suffering created by the civil war in Somalia. But it soon became

9. U.S. Marines landed in Haiti on September 19, 1994, to restore President Jean-Bertrand Aristide and quell civil strife.

10. Karl von Clausewitz (1780–1831), Prussian general and military theorist. In *On War* (1833) he wrote that "War is...a continuation of political relations...by other means."

clear that the humanitarian effort could not enjoy long-term success without a return to civil order. And no internal force was available to supply this.

Hence, the intervention created a painful choice: either the UN would make Somalia into a colony and spend decades engaged in "nation-building"; or the UN forces would eventually withdraw and Somalia revert to its prior anarchy. Since America and the UN were unwilling to govern Somalia for thirty years, it followed that the job of feeding the hungry and helping the sick must be left to civilian aid agencies and private charities.

Conclusion: military intervention without an attainable purpose creates as many problems as it solves.

This was further demonstrated in the former Yugoslavia, where early action to arm the victims of aggression so that they could defend themselves would have been far more effective than the UN's half-hearted, multilateral intervention. A neutral peacekeeping operation, lightly armed, in an area where there was no peace to keep, served mainly to consolidate the gains from aggression. Eventually, the UN peacekeepers became hostages, used by the aggressor to deter more effective action against him.[11] All in all, a sorry episode, ended by the Croatian army, NATO airpower and American diplomacy.[12]

The combined effect of interventions in Bosnia, Somalia and, indeed, Rwanda[13] has been to shake the self-confidence of key Western powers and to tarnish the reputation of the UN. And now a dangerous trend is evident: as the Haiti case shows, the Security Council seems increasingly prepared to widen the legal basis for intervention. We are

11. The Bosnian Serbs detained 377 UN personnel as hostages against NATO air strikes between May 26 and June 18, 1995.
12. Croatia retook the Krajina region from the Serbs in August 1995. From August 30 to September 14, NATO subjected the Bosnian Serbs to sustained air attacks in "Operation Deliberate Force." A ceasefire took effect on October 5. Peace talks opened at Dayton, Ohio, on November 1 and ended in agreement on November 21, 1995.
13. Large-scale ethnic violence erupted in Rwanda in April 1994, leading to the deaths of over 200,000 people and the displacement of some five million. Neither a UN presence nor French intervention from June to September 1994 made much impact on the situation.

seeing, in fact, that classically dangerous combination—a growing disproportion between theoretical claims and practical means.

Compare this hubris with the failure to act effectively against the proliferation of nuclear, chemical and biological weapons, and the means to deliver them. As I have already argued, these are falling into dangerous hands.

Given the intellectual climate in the West today, it is probably unrealistic to expect military intervention to remove the source of the threat, as for example against North Korea—except perhaps when the offender invites us to do so by invading a small neighbouring country. Even then, as we now know, our success in destroying Saddam's nuclear and chemical weapons capability was limited.

And we cannot be sure that the efforts by inspectors of the International Atomic Energy Authority to prevent Saddam putting civil nuclear power to military uses have been any more successful; indeed, we may reasonably suspect that they have not.

What then can we do? There is no mysterious diplomatic means to disarm a state which is not willing to be disarmed. As Frederick the Great[14] mordantly observed: "Diplomacy without arms is like music without instruments." Arms control and non-proliferation measures have a role in restraining rogue states, but only when combined with other measures.

If America and its allies cannot deal with the problem directly by pre-emptive military means, they must at least diminish the incentive for the Saddams, the Gaddafis and others to acquire new weapons in the first place. That means the West must install effective ballistic missile defence which would protect us and our armed forces, reduce or even nullify the rogue state's arsenal, and enable us to retaliate.

So the potential contribution of ballistic missile defence to peace and stability seems to me to be very great.

—First and most obviously, it promises the possibility of protection

14. Frederick II (1712–1786), King of Prussia 1740–1786.

if deterrence fails; or if there is a limited and unauthorized use of nuclear missiles.

—Second, it would also preserve the capability of the West to project its power overseas.

—Third, it would diminish the dangers of one country overturning the regional balance of power by acquiring these weapons.

—Fourth, it would strengthen our existing deterrent against a hostile nuclear superpower by preserving the West's powers of retaliation.

—And fifth, it would enhance diplomacy's power to restrain proliferation by diminishing the utility of offensive systems.

Acquiring an effective global defence against ballistic missiles is therefore a matter of the greatest importance and urgency. But the risk is that thousands of people may be killed by an attack which forethought and wise preparation might have prevented.

It is, of course, often the case in foreign affairs that statesmen are dealing with problems for which there is no ready solution. They must manage them as best they can.

## THE EUROPEAN UNION AND CENTRAL EUROPE

That might be true of nuclear proliferation, but no such excuses can be made for the European Union's activities at the end of the Cold War. It faced a task so obvious and achievable as to count as an almost explicit duty laid down by history: namely, the speedy incorporation of the new Central European democracies—Poland, Hungary and what was then Czechoslovakia—within the EU's economic and political structures.

Early entry into Europe was the wish of the new democracies; it would help to stabilize them politically and smooth their transition to market economies; and it would ratify the post–Cold War settlement in Europe. Given the stormy past of that region—the inhabitants are said to produce more history than they can consume locally —everyone should have wished to see it settled economically and politically inside a stable European structure.

Why was this not done? Why was every obstacle put in the way of the new market democracies? Why were their exports subject to the kind of absurd quotas that have until now been reserved for Japan? And why is there still no room at the inn?

The answer is that the European Union was too busy contemplating its own navel. Both the Commission and a majority of member Governments were committed to an early "deepening" of the EU (that is, centralizing more power in the EU's supranational institutions), and they felt that a "widening" of it (that is, admitting new members) would complicate, obstruct or even prevent this process.

So, while the "deepening" went ahead, they arranged to keep the Central Europeans out by the diplomat's favourite tactic: negotiations to admit them. In making this decision, the European Union put extravagant and abstract schemes ahead of practical necessities, in the manner of doctrinaire "projectors" from Jonathan Swift[15] down to the present.

And with the usual disastrous results. The "visionary" schemes of "deepening" either have failed or are failing.

The "fixed" exchange rates of the European Exchange Rate Mechanism have made the yo-yo seem like a symbol of rigidity; they crashed in and out of it in September 1992 and have shown no signs of obeying the diktats of Brussels since then.

The next stage of monetary union agreed at Maastricht—the single currency—is due in 1999, when member states will have to achieve strict budgetary criteria. With three years to go, only Luxemburg fully meets these tests; the attempts by other countries to meet them on time have pushed up unemployment, hiked interest rates, depressed economic activity, and created civil unrest.

And for what? Across the continent businessmen and bankers increasingly question the *economic* need for a single currency at all. It is essentially a political symbol—the currency of a European state and people which don't actually exist, except perhaps in the mind of a Brussels bureaucrat.

Yet these symbols were pursued at a real political cost in Central Europe. The early enthusiasm for the West and Western institutions began to wane. Facing tariff barriers and quotas in Western Europe,

---

15. Jonathan Swift (1667–1745), Irish satirist, political journalist and churchman, whose works include *A Tale of a Tub* (1704) and *Gulliver's Travels* (1726).

the Central Europeans began to erect their own. And those politicians who had bravely pursued tough-minded policies of economic reform, believing that they were following the advice of European leaders, found themselves left in the lurch when the going got rough. Only the Czech Republic under the leadership of Vaclav Klaus[16] has remained on course to a normal society.

In the last few years, the democratic reformers have fallen one by one in the former communist satellites, to be replaced by neo-communist Governments promising the impossible: transition to a market economy without tears. This is a tragedy in itself, and an avoidable one. But with Russia lurching politically into a more authoritarian nationalist course, and the question of Central Europe's membership of NATO still unsettled, it has more than merely economic implications.

## NATO

Which brings me to my last example of institutional failure, mercifully a partial one counterbalanced by some successes, namely NATO. NATO is a very fine military instrument; it won the Cold War when it had a clear military doctrine. But an instrument cannot define its own purposes, and since the dissolution of the Warsaw Pact, Western statesmen have found it difficult to give NATO a clear one.

Indeed, they have shilly-shallied on the four major questions facing the Alliance:

—Should Russia be regarded as a potential threat or a partner? (Russia may be about to answer that in a clearer fashion than we would like.)

—Should NATO turn its attention to "out-of-area," where most of the post–Cold War threats, such as nuclear proliferation, now lie?

—Should NATO admit the new democracies of Central Europe as full members with full responsibilities as quickly as prudently possible?

—Should Europe develop its own "defence identity" in NATO, even though this is a concept driven entirely by politics and has damaging military implications?

16. Vaclav Klaus (born 1941), Czech economist and politician. Finance minister 1989–1992; Prime Minister 1992–1997.

Such questions tend to be decided not in the abstract, not at inter-governmental conferences convened to look into the crystal ball, but on the anvil of necessity in the heat of crisis. And that is exactly what happened in the long-running crisis over Bosnia.

At first, the supporters of a European foreign policy and a European defence identity declared the former Yugoslavia "Europe's crisis" and asked the US to keep out. The US was glad to do so. But the European Union's farcical involvement only made matters worse and, after a while, was effectively abandoned.

Then the United Nations became involved, and asked NATO to be its military agent in its peacekeeping operations.

Finally, when the UN-NATO personnel were taken hostage, the US intervened, employed NATO airpower with real effect, forced the combatants to the conference table, for better or worse imposed an agreement on them, and now heads a large NATO contingent that is enforcing it.

In the course of stamping its authority on events, the US also stamped its authority on the European members of NATO. And since the logistical supply chain goes through Hungary, it drew the Central Europeans into NATO operations in a small way. Whether NATO will apply the logic of this crisis in future strategic planning remains to be seen; but for the armchair theorists of a closed, passive and divided NATO, Bosnia has been no end of a lesson.

These various institutional failures are worrying enough in their own terms and in our own times. If we look ahead still further to the end of the twenty-first century, however, an alarming and unstable future is on the cards.


## THE WEST AND THE REST

Consider the number of medium-to-large states in the world that have now embarked on a free market revolution: India, China, Brazil, possibly Russia. Add to these the present economic great powers: the USA and Japan, and, if the federalists get their way, a European superstate with its own independent foreign and defence policy separate from, and perhaps inimical to, the United States. What we see here in 2096 is an unstable world in which there are more than half a dozen "great powers," all with their own clients, all vulnerable if they stand alone, all capable of increasing their power and influence if they form the right kind of alliance, and all engaged willy-nilly in perpetual diplomatic manoeuvres to ensure that their relative positions improve rather than deteriorate. In other words, 2096 might look like 1914 played on a somewhat larger stage.

That need not come to pass if the Atlantic Alliance remains as it is today: in essence, America as the dominant power surrounded by allies which generally follow its lead. Such are the realities of population, resources, technology and capital that if America remains the dominant partner in a united West, and militarily engaged in Europe, then the West can continue to be the dominant power in the world as a whole.

## What Is to Be Done?

I believe that what is now required is a new and imaginative Atlantic initiative. Its purpose must be to redefine Atlanticism in the light of the challenges I have been describing. There are rare moments when history is open and its course changed by means such as these. We may be at just such a moment now.

### REVIVING THE ALLIANCE

First, security. As my discussion of the Bosnian crisis demonstrated, the key lies in two reforms: opening NATO membership to Poland, Hungary and the Czech Republic; and extending NATO's role so that it is able to operate out-of-area.

Both reforms will require a change in NATO's existing procedures. An attack on the territory of one member must, of course, continue to be regarded unambiguously as an attack on that of all; but that principle of universality need not apply to out-of-area activities. Indeed, it needs to be recognized that a wider role for NATO cannot be achieved if every member state has to participate in an out-of-area operation before it can go ahead. What is required are flexible arrangements which, to use a fashionable phrase, permit the creation of "coalitions of the willing."

Would NATO expansion mark a new division of Europe and give Russia the right to intervene in states outside the fold? Not in the least. Among other reasons, we could hold out the possibility of admitting those countries which subsequently demonstrate a commitment to democratic values and which have trained military forces up to an acceptable standard. That would be a powerful incentive for such states to pursue the path of democratic reform and defence preparedness.

NATO also provides the best available mechanism for co-ordinating the contribution of America's allies to a global system of ballistic missile defence: that is, one providing protection against missile attack from whatever source it comes.

If, however, the United States is to build this global ballistic defence system with its allies, it needs the assurance that the Alliance is a permanent one resting on the solid foundations of American leadership. That raises, in my view, very serious doubts about the currently fashionable idea of a separate European "defence identity" within the Alliance.

Essentially, this is another piece of political symbolism, associated among European federalists with long-term aspirations for a European state with its own foreign and defence policy. It would create the armed forces of a country which does not exist. But, like the single currency, it would have damaging practical consequences in the here and now.

In the first place, it contains the germs of a major future transatlantic rift. And in the second, it has no military rationale or benefits. Indeed, it has potentially severe military drawbacks. Even a French General admitted that during the Gulf War the US forces were "the eyes and ears" of the French troops. Without America, NATO is a political talking shop, not a military force.

Nor is that likely to be changed in any reasonably foreseeable circumstances. Defence expenditure has been falling sharply in almost all European states in recent years. Even if this process were now halted and reversed, it would take many years before Europe could hope to replace what America presently makes available to the Alliance by way of command and control facilities, airlift capacity, surveillance and sheer firepower. Defence policy cannot be built upon political symbolism and utopian projects of nation-building which ignore or even defy military logic and fiscal prudence.

### TRANSATLANTIC FREE TRADE

But even a vigorous and successful NATO would not survive indefinitely in a West divided along the lines of trade and economics. One of the great threats to Atlantic unity in recent years has been the succession of trade wars, ranging from steel to pasta, which have strained relations across the Atlantic. So the second element of a new Atlantic initiative must take the form of a concerted programme to liberalize trade, thereby stimulating growth and creating badly needed new jobs. More specifically, we need to move towards a Transatlantic Free Trade Area, uniting the North American Free Trade Area with a European Union enlarged to incorporate the Central European countries.

I realize that this may not seem the most propitious moment in American politics to advocate a new trade agreement. But the arguments against free trade between advanced industrial countries and poor Third World ones—even if I accepted them, which I do not—certainly do not apply to a Transatlantic Free Trade deal.

Such a trade bloc would unite countries with similar incomes and levels of regulation. It would therefore involve much less disruption and temporary job loss, while still bringing significant gains in efficiency and prosperity. This has been recognized by American labour unions, notably by Mr. Lane Kirkland[17] in a series of important speeches. And it would create a trade bloc of unparalleled wealth (and therefore influence) in world trade negotiations.

Of course, economic gains are only half of the argument for a TAFTA. It would also provide a solid economic underpinning to America's continued military commitment to Europe, while strengthening the still-fragile economies and political structures of Central

17. Joseph Lane Kirkland (1922–1999), US trade unionist. President of the American Federation of Labor/Congress of Industrial Organizations (AFL-CIO) 1979–1995.

Europe. It would be, in effect, the economic equivalent of NATO and, as such, the second pillar of Atlantic unity under American leadership.

## POLITICAL FOUNDATIONS

Yet, let us never forget that there is a third pillar—the political one.

The West is not just some Cold War construct, devoid of significance in today's freer, more fluid world. It rests upon distinctive values and virtues, ideas and ideals, and above all upon a common experience of liberty.

True, the Asia Pacific may be fast becoming the new centre of global economic power. Quite rightly, both the United States and Britain take an ever closer interest in developments there.

But it is the West—above all, perhaps, the English-speaking peoples of the West—that has formed that system of liberal democracy which is politically dominant and which we all know offers the best hope of global peace and prosperity. In order to uphold these things, the Atlantic political relationship must be constantly nurtured and renewed.

So we must breathe new life into the consultative political institutions of the West such as the Atlantic Council and the North Atlantic Assembly.[18] All too often, they lack influence and presence in public debate. Above all, however—loath as I am to suggest another gathering of international leaders—I would propose an annual summit of the Heads of Government of all the North Atlantic countries, under the chairmanship of the President of the United States.

What all this adds up to is *not* another supranational entity. That would be unwieldy and unworkable. It is something more subtle, but I hope more durable: a form of Atlantic partnership which attempts to solve common problems while respecting the sovereignty of the member states. In the course of identifying those problems

18. The Atlantic Council is the British section of the Atlantic Treaty Association, which was founded in 1954 to promote the objectives and ideas of NATO in all its member states. The North Atlantic Assembly was established in 1955 as the Conference of Members of Parliament from NATO Member Countries to strengthen co-operation and understanding within the alliance and foster a common feeling of Atlantic solidarity. It was renamed in 1966.

and co-operating to solve them, Governments would gradually discover that they were shaping an Atlantic public opinion and political consciousness.

## Fifty Years On

The reaction, fifty years ago, to that earlier Fulton speech was swift, dramatic and, at first, highly critical. Indeed, to judge from the critics, you would have imagined that it was not Stalin but Churchill who had drawn down the Iron Curtain.

But for all the immediate disharmony, it soon became evident that Fulton had struck a deeper chord. It resulted in a decisive shift in opinion: by May, the opinion polls recorded that 83 percent of Americans now favoured the idea of a permanent alliance between the United States and Britain, which was subsequently broadened into NATO.

By speaking as and when he did, Churchill guarded against a repetition of the withdrawal of America from Europe which, after 1919, allowed the instability to emerge that plunged the whole world—including America—into a second war.

Like my uniquely distinguished predecessor, I too may be accused of alarmism in pointing to new dangers to which present institutions —and attitudes—are proving unequal. But, also like him, I have every confidence in the resources and the values of the Western civilization we are defending.

In particular, I believe (to use Churchill's words) that: "If all British moral and material forces and convictions are joined with your own in fraternal association, the highroads of the future will be clear, not only for us but for all, not only for our time, but for a century to come."

That at least has not changed in fifty years.

〜 LARRY P. ARNN is President of the Claremont Institute. He studied in England from 1977 to 1980, serving as director of research for Martin Gilbert, official biographer of Winston Churchill. He regularly publishes articles and essays on politics, foreign policy, and economics. He is a member of the Board of Academic Advisers to the Churchill Center. His chapter originally appeared in the *Weekly Standard* 1:24 (March 4, 1996): 25–28, copyright News America, Inc., and is reprinted with permission.

〜 WINSTON S. CHURCHILL (1874–1965), Prime Minister of Britain from 1940 to 1945 and from 1951 to 1955, delivered his "Iron Curtain" speech, "The Sinews of Peace," at Westminster College in Fulton, Missouri, on March 5, 1946. The text of the speech in the prologue of this book and quotations from Churchill's speeches and writings in subsequent chapters are reproduced with permission of Curtis Brown, Ltd., London, on behalf of the estate of Sir Winston S. Churchill; the copyright of the speech and quotations is held by Winston S. Churchill.

〜 DANIEL J. MAHONEY is Associate Professor of Political Science at Assumption College in Worcester, Massachusetts. He is author of *The Liberal Political Science of Raymond Aron* (1992) and *De Gaulle: Statesmanship, Grandeur, and Modern Democracy* (1996), and editor of and author of an introductory essay to Pierre Manent, *Modern Liberty and Its Discontents* (1998). He is currently completing a book on the political thought of Aleksandr Solzhenitsyn. Professor Mahoney is grateful to the Earhart Foundation for its continuing support of his research and writing on statesmanship.

↪ JAMES W. MULLER is Professor of Political Science at the University of Alaska, Anchorage, where he has taught since 1983. He is editor of *Churchill as Peacemaker* (1997) and *The Revival of Constitutionalism* (1988), and is working on a book about Churchill's writings. Winner of the Farrow Award for Excellence in Churchill Studies (1995), Professor Muller is a Governor of the Churchill Center and Chairman of its Board of Academic Advisers.

↪ PATRICK J. C. POWERS is Adjunct Professor of Philosophy at Anna Maria College in Paxton, Massachusetts, and Senior Research Analyst on health care legislation for the Gartner Group of Stamford, Connecticut. Professor Powers has written about political philosophy from Plato to the present and is preparing a book, *Winston Churchill's Statesmanship: Lessons for Liberal Democracy.* He is a member of the Board of Academic Advisers to the Churchill Center.

↪ PAUL A. RAHE is Jay P. Walker Professor of History at the University of Tulsa. His areas of specialization and research include ancient history, early-modern political thought, and the American Revolution. His massive work *Republics Ancient and Modern*, first published in 1992, has been reissued in a three-volume paperback edition. Professor Rahe is a member of the Board of Academic Advisers to the Churchill Center.

↪ JOHN RAMSDEN, Head of the Department of History at Queen Mary and Westfield College, London, was Robertson Visiting Professor of British History at Westminster College in 1995–1996. Author of many books on British politics in the twentieth century, he is at work on a book about Churchill's postwar political reputation. Professor Ramsden is a member of the Board of Academic Advisers to the Churchill Center.

↪ MARGARET THATCHER, Prime Minister of Britain from 1979 to 1990, came to Westminster College on March 9, 1996, to deliver the John Findley Green Foundation lecture, "New Threats for Old," fifty years after Winston Churchill's "Iron Curtain" speech. The text of the lecture in the epilogue of this book is reprinted by permission of HarperCollins Publishers, Ltd., from *The Collected Speeches of Margaret Thatcher*, ed. Robin Harris (New York: HarperCollins, 1997), 588–604; notes were originally prepared by Mr. Harris and, in some cases, brought up to date by the editor of this book.

᠙ SPENCER WARREN is President of the Insider's Washington Experience, a public-policy seminar program. He was formerly a member of the Policy Planning Staff at the U.S. Department of State and served as counsel to members of both houses of Congress. His articles on public and cultural affairs have been published in the *National Interest* and other journals and newspapers.

# Index